Stephan's Journey
A Sojourn into Freedom

by
Lillian Belinfante Herzberg

Lillian Belinfante Herzberg

PublishAmerica

Baltimore

© 2003 by Lillian Belinfante Herzberg.
All rights reserved. No part of this book may be reproduced, stored in a retrieval system, or transmitted in any form or by any means without the prior written permission of the publishers, except by a reviewer who may quote brief passages in a review to be printed in a newspaper, magazine, or journal.

First printing

ISBN: 1-4137-0275-9
PUBLISHED BY PUBLISHAMERICA, LLLP
www.publishamerica.com
Baltimore

Printed in the United States of America

*For Stephan who lived it
and for his children
who didn't have to.*

Acknowledgments

I am appreciative of the encouragement my wonderful supportive writers' group gave to me, and they are worth mentioning: Harold Aster, Karl Bell, Peter Berkos, Nancy Canfield, Bessie Fantl, Rosalie Kramer, Sonia Rosenberg and Morry Shechet, who critique with loving care.

I particularly value the support my husband, Ernie, continues to give me.

Chapter One

My father once told me my mother had been warned that a pregnancy could kill her. Allowing that, no one could have predicted that my hazardous birth foreshadowed the struggle I was to experience in the future, just so I could exist. Actually, it was a miracle that I was even born.

My father, Arthur Lewy, was an uncommonly strict disciplinarian. He once hit me so hard I felt the pain for a week. I can still remember how it sounded when his hand connected with my skin.

As I grew older, when I did something wrong, that hand of his was there, quicker than lightening. Sometimes when I transgressed, he slapped me across the face with the back of his hand just hard enough for me to feel the sting for a long time without leaving a mark.

As an only child, not having a sibling's experience to which I could compare my existence, I grew up believing my father's conduct was standard behavior for parents toward their children. At the time I did not realize I was being prepared for my future which, perhaps, was his intent all the time, but neither of us realized just what the future held for us. But then, my father always had a life that demanded much of him.

"Your name and age?" the superintendent of Auerbach Orphanage asked nine- year-old Arthur Lewy who stood mute, too frightened to answer.

"He's nine years old," answered the woman who worked for the offices of the Jewish Charitable Organization, and who had brought him.

7

"What's his story?" the man in charged asked, ignoring the shaking child standing before him.

"As far as we know, he was born in 1893, one of nine children."

"And where is his family now?

"His parents and seven of his siblings are dead, the cause of their death a mystery. Only he and his four-year-old brother now survive."

"Yes, well, his brother is too young to qualify for admittance to the orphanage."

"That's all right. We have already placed the child with a nice family."

Auerbach, the Jewish orphanage located in Berlin, operated on a system similar to the German military style. In the cold, rigid environment of the institution, the children were dressed in uniforms and helmets resembling those of the Berlin police force.

During the years in the orphanage, Arthur lost track of his younger brother. Much later, during World War II, he learned his brother had died in a Nazi concentration camp.

By 1909, a somber, repressed, lonely sixteen-year-old young man, Arthur was now eligible to leave the orphanage. He was called into the superintendent's office, where the rotund middle aged man, sitting behind the huge oak desk, spoke in a condescending tone, "Your teachers have informed me you qualified for the university, Arthur. Life goes on after school, you know; therefore, you should have a plan for your future."

"I will have to give it some thought, sir," he answered.

"Very good. I hope you have learned something here in Auerbach that will see you through life. Good luck."

And so he left the place that had been a roof over his head for seven years.

In 1914, after attending college, he was drafted into the German army. Arthur's war experiences both sickened him and hardened him. Life in the trenches was deplorable. *Does anyone ever get used to the stink of the dead decaying bodies defiling the air?* he wondered. The ever present rats added to his misery. Keeping dry, especially in areas when they neared Belgium, was impossible. He spent much of his time scraping the muck off of his shoes and pants.

The army was using a new weapon, a flame thrower, which shot out a stream of burning fuel. The sight of the horror it inflicted made Arthur put his feelings into an imaginary steel case hidden deep inside his soul so he wouldn't imagine the pain that was being inflicted. Both the users and the target became casualties.

Except during an attack, life, if one could call it that, was routine and dull. "I don't know which is worse," Arthur told Ziggy, his new army friend, "the fighting or the monotony."

One night Ziggy and Arthur were assigned to repair the trenches by packing the sides with mud. "I think boredom is a better situation than this," Ziggy whispered in desperation to Arthur. "One could get killed here."

Arthur didn't disagree.

As soldiers, they stood guard or checked telephone lines, or brought food from behind the battle lines. At night, on patrol, they repaired the barbed wire. Meanwhile officers tried to gather information about the enemy.

In April, 1915, in the Second Battle of Ypres, the German army used poison gas for the first time against the Allies. Fortunately, at that period, Arthur had been assigned a clerical job at the rear of the fighting. His friend Ziggy was not so fortunate. Lucky to escape himself, Ziggy saw what the gas did when the wind changed, causing their own soldiers vomit from the gas or be asphyxiated. Sometimes both.

In 1918, the Germans shifted their forces from the Eastern Front to the Western Front. In spring, Germany began to stage three offensives. Arthur and Ziggy were in the middle of the fighting.

General Ludendorff hoped to deliver a devastating blow to the Allies before the Americans could reach the front. On March 21, 1918, Germany attacked St. Quentin, a city in the Somme River Valley. By March 26, British troops were on the retreat.

Later in March, the Germans began to bombard Paris. "Big Berthas," the German's gigantic guns, were capable of hurling their shells up to 75 miles away.

Arthur had no enthusiasm for war, as did the superior officers. Unhappily, he took part in the second German offensive beginning on April 9, along the Lys River in Belgium. "Thank God General Ludendorff finally called off the attack," Arthur told the soldier fighting next to him. "We may survive this war yet."

A month later, on May 27th, Germany attacked a third time near the Aisne River. By May 30, German troops had reached the Marne River.

"In spite of our advances, I don't think we're going to win this one," Arthur's Commanding Officer said, taking his men into his confidence. "So try not to get killed."

"I hope Ludendorff realizes Germany can no longer overcome the superiority of the Allies before we are all killed," Arthur added in his quiet way.

The Officer was right. The turning point to end World War I was the Second Battle of Marne. Shortly after the armistice was signed, Arthur and Ziggy were transferred back to Berlin where they were discharged. Arthur resolved never to pick up a weapon again.

In 1919, a short time after he was discharged from the army, his old army buddy asked him to a dinner party at his home. He was about to refuse the invitation.

"Thanks just the same, Ziggy, but I'm not much for socializing."

"Oh, come on. The food will be a hell of a lot better than the slop they gave us in the army."

"Well…" he hesitated. "All right. I'll be there."

Arthur was surprised when he arrived at Ziggy's residence. It was located in the more affluent section of Berlin. He realized Ziggy was way out of his league economically. He thought as he stood at the front door, *Maybe I should have stuck to my guns and refused his invitation.* But it was too late. Ziggy opened the door before Arthur rang the bell.

"Great to see you again, old man. Glad you could come."

Arthur was handed a drink by the man passing them around. As he sipped the liquid, he looked around in admiration. Ziggy had never let on that he came from a wealthy family and always treated Arthur as an equal.

"Dinner is served," a maid said quietly to the twelve people gathered in the parlor, and they all moved into the dining room.

"You sit here, Arthur, next to my friend Gertrude."

He sat down next to a charming young woman dressed in pale gray chiffon, who, by the end of the evening, captured his heart. She often told her friends they fell in love between the tomato soup and the apple strudel.

A few months later while holding her hand, Arthur told Gertrude, "I still cannot believe my good fortune that you are willing to marry me. What do you see in such a somber, solitary fellow as I?"

She touched his face. "It is your beautiful blue eyes."

"Are you really sure you want to do this?"

"Yes, I am sure. Come, no more excuses. I want you to go with me to Alt Glienicke and meet my parents and two brothers."

"Alt Glienicke?"

"Yes, it's a small but lovely village. It's easy to get to since it is quite near Berlin. Oh, one more thing you should know. As a very young man my father was struck by lightening, and lost his ability to hear and speak. He does read lips, however, but my mother usually speaks for him."

They got off the train at Adlershof. After a brief bus ride, it was only a short walk to where Gertrude once lived with her loving family.

"The sun is shining, and the weather is just right. I hope it is a good omen," Arthur said.

"Don't be nervous, my love. Everything will be fine."

As they approached the village, Arthur walked into a world new to him. "The houses all look alike, except for the colors," he said in amazement. The two story house in which the Puls lived was in the midst of similar homes. "Even the small front gardens look the same."

"Ah, but if you look closely, the Puls garden is much prettier, don't you think?"

They opened the front gate and walked up the path to the wooden, ornately carved door. When Gertrude turned the knob, the door opened, much to the astonishment of her city bred suitor.

"You don't lock your doors here?"

"No need, my love. No one does it."

They were greeted in the front hall by Frau Puls. "Right on time." Then directing Arthur to a door on the left, she said imperiously, "You can wash up in there, Herr Lewy."

They were seated in a formal dining room with the large window overlooking the back garden.

"This is a lovely room," Arthur told Frau Puls, not knowing what else to say.

Almost immediately, the maid served the first course. Gertrude introduced Arthur to her two brothers, Ewald, her younger brother, who worked in his father's upholstery business, and Herman, her older brother, who worked as an engineer for the A.G. Farben Company. They all sat around the dining room table eating in silence.

The frigid atmosphere in the Puls home and the cool reception Arthur received made Puls' displeasure at their daughter's choice for a husband dramatically obvious to Arthur. Frau Puls, dressed entirely in black, as if in mourning, emphasized the family's feelings unquestionably.

"Shall we adjourn into the sitting room for our coffee?" she asked as she arose from the table. The maid had already started to clear the table. They all followed her into the parlor.

As Frau Puls sat down on the plush dark blue sofa, she started to pour the coffee from a silver pot and first handed the Meissen china cup to her husband, then to Arthur before she started to speak.

"Excuse me, Herr Lewy, I do not want to appear rude…"

Arthur waited for the "but."

"But," Gertrude's mother continued, as she filled her cup nearly full and placed it on the glass coffee table in front of her, "Your backgrounds are so very dissimilar. I am fearful there might be some difficulties." She then took a bite of cookie.

Arthur knew to what she referred.

Before Arthur could speak, Gertrude said quietly, facing her father so he could read her lips, "We have already considered that, and to overcome any religious differences, we have agreed any son we might have will be brought up Jewish, and any daughter will be raised Protestant."

Gertrude then moved from her seat beside Arthur and went to sit next to her mother. "Mutti," she said, while still looking at her father as she spoke, "We prefer you and Papa give us your blessings, but I want you to know my mind is made up, and no matter what, we are definitely going to marry."

Her parents realized they were defeated, and rather than lose their only daughter, they reluctantly gave their blessings.

The wedding took place a short time later in the City Hall, and a small reception was held in a quaint little restaurant nearby with only the Puls family present.

The newlyweds settled on the third floor at 46 Köepenicker Strasse, Arthur's tiny, four room apartment in Berlin.

"I'm so sorry I cannot afford more at the moment, my dear, but I hope to be able to provide a larger place before too long," Arthur told Gertrude when they climbed the stairs to their flat.

"Arthur, don't apologize...ever. We'll be just fine."

She looked around the apartment. "What lovely blue tiled Kachel Ofen these rooms have," she said smiling with approval. She was referring to the ceiling high heaters each room had which would provide their warmth. "These will make us quite comfortable during the winter cold. Yes, this looks as if it will be quite comfortable."

"You'll have to get used to the bathroom being on a landing seven steps up. We share it with three other families, and using it during the morning might become complicated since everyone seems to need it at the same time."

"We'll manage," she said with a slight smile.

In one of the small rooms, she noticed a wall covered with maps which her new husband used for astrological studies. She looked puzzled.

When he noticed her facial expression, he told her, "I am a firm believer in the stars."

Arthur never mentioned what he saw in the stars to his son. Much later, Stephan was to learn what the stars had revealed.

On their first Friday night together, Gertrude prepared the traditional Sabbath meal, chicken soup, roasted chicken, boiled potatoes and a cooked vegetable. The aroma from the onions and chicken spread throughout the apartment and seeped down the stairs to greet Arthur and tease his senses when he came home. He was extravagant with his compliments. In turn, she was delighted at how pleased he was, and full of questions, eager to do the right things.

A week or two later, on Sunday morning, as Arthur sat at his desk, Gertrude brought him a cup of coffee and noticed he was absorbed in thought.

"What are you doing, my love, that causes such a frown this fine sunny Sunday morning?"

"I'm trying to figure out how much tax we must give to the government this year to support the Jewish community."

"I do not understand," she said as she went behind his chair and looked over his shoulder. "Why do we have to pay a percentage of your income to support the Jewish community if we do not belong to any Jewish organization?"

"All people, no matter what religion, are required by the German government to support and maintain their hospitals, orphanages, churches, priests, ministers and rabbis."

"Even those of us who only have a cultural attachment, and observe none of the holy days, like we, except for the Sabbath, of course?"

"I'm afraid so," Arthur said, smiling in approval at her question. "I'm sure your father paid this tax annually."

This was all new to Gertrude who admired and adored her new husband. She had led a rather sheltered life, and so accepted his explanations as she did anything he told her. They had all the appearance of being an ideally happy couple.

Chapter Two

Arthur had a busy day in the tobacco shop he owned and looked forward to coming home for the midday meal with his precious Gertrude. He called to her as he usually did when he opened the front door.

"Gertrude, I'm home."

There was no response. He called again and started toward their bedroom when he heard a groan.

"Gertrude, where are you? Are you playing a game?" As he followed the sound, he found Gertrude lying helplessly on their bed.

"What is it, Liebchen."

She could hardly speak. Her face was red. Her lips were dry and cracked. She managed to croak out the words, "I do not feel at all well. My throat is sore, and I think I have a high fever."

Before he called the doctor, he rushed to apply cold cloths to her forehead, hoping to make her feel more comfortable. Seated by the bed, he waited impatiently for the physician to come. He did not return to his store for the remainder of the day.

It was Arthur's habit to exercise control over his emotions and to manipulate the activities surrounding him. Now he felt helpless and tortured seeing his wife's discomfort, unable to ease her pain. The doctor diagnosed the illness almost at once.

"I am afraid Frau Lewy has come down with a streptococcal infection, Herr Lewy. There seems to be quite a few cases in Berlin right now."

After the doctor told them the diagnosis, Arthur was frantic. "What can we do?"

"Just keep her quiet until the fever subsides. Other than that, we can do nothing. I only hope it does not develop into rheumatic fever."

But it did.

Finally, after nearly two weeks in bed, the fever tapered off and Gertrude's health started to improve. However, she had difficulty walking up and down the stairs to their apartment. The climb left her gasping, short of breath, and with sharp pains in her chest.

Finally, Arthur told her, "Gertrude, I hate seeing you this way. We must see another physician. Maybe he can help."

The new doctor told the couple what they dreaded to hear.

"I am afraid your heart has been affected, Frau Lewy. And from what the condition of your heart indicates, I am sad to tell you it will be impossible for you to carry a child to term, let alone experience the rigors of childbirth without serious consequences to your life. Yes, yes, much too dangerous for you to bear a child."

On their way home, Arthur said in a stern sounding voice Gertrude had never heard him use. "Under no circumstances will we endanger your health…your life, to have a baby. No!"

"But…"

"No buts. I would rather die myself than lose you."

And so it was decided—no children.

Gertrude had nearly recovered when she started feeling ill once more. Her appetite deteriorated, and when she was able to eat, she could barely keep the food down. Finally, Arthur insisted she return to the doctor's office.

After the doctor examined her, she and Arthur went into his office. The doctor's face was grim. "I believe I told you before, Frau Lewy, it would be impossible for you to complete a pregnancy, let alone experience the rigors of childbirth, without serious consequences to your life. Well, I find you are pregnant, and the consequences might be very serious. Now, it is possible…"

Gertrude interrupted and raised her chin defiantly. "I'm going to have this baby. I'm going to have a son, and we are both going to survive," she informed the concerned physician and her anxious husband.

It was touch and go for a while. She had to spend weeks at a time in bed. Her legs swelled. Her eyesight blurred every so often. She could hardly hold food down the entire first trimester. Her mother wanted her to go to Alt Glienicke, but Gertrude refused.

"My place is here with the father of my child," she told her family.

When her time came, her labor was excruciating. She tossed and turned, writhing in pain. Hours passed. Her perspiration dampened and stained the bedding. The doctor warned Arthur to stay out of the room, but he insisted he stay.

"We should not have done this, Liebchen."

"Too late to change our mind," she joked between moans.

True to her word, and with great difficulty, she gave birth to a healthy son, Heinz Stephan. It was March 11, 1925.

One of my earliest memories is of my mother saying the blessing over the Sabbath candles every Friday night, and hearing my father follow with a blessing over the bread and wine before we ate our special Sabbath dinner together.

One Friday night guests joined us for the Sabbath dinner. I probably was no older than three. My father yelled at me in front of our guests. "Don't you know the proper way to hold your knife and fork?" No doubt he was trying to teach me table manners.

I remember his eyes narrowed, and he scowled. Then he took the steel handle of the knife, bent it slightly, and let it snap on my cheek. The pain traveled all the way down to my feet. I'm sure I must have screamed. Beside the physical pain, I felt humiliated.

Others at the table avoided looking at me, their eyes glued to their plates.

And when I looked for help from my mother, I could see her flinch, but she never said a word, at least not in front of me. If my mother saw any of this, she turned her head away. I like to think she believed if she did not see it, it did not happen, and she did not have to deal with it. I know it must have hurt her. It was not the way she was brought up.

After I was born, my mother had to spend more and more time in bed. When I was old enough to appreciate it, we both took great delight in her reading to me. We often ate our meals together. She showed me a great deal of affection. I remember she hugged me, kissed me and praised me when I did something well. We had some loving and wonderful mother-son moments. As I grew older, she remained bedridden much of the time. Yet, it seemed she was constantly there for me. All and all, not withstanding my father's harsh dicipline, I remember having a warm and loving family life, although short lived.

I always wanted to do little things for her, things she could not do for herself. I thought if I helped enough, she would get better. When she wanted anything, I told her, "I'll get it. I'll get it for you, Mutti," and I ran off seeking the object she wanted.

If I deserved it, she spanked me. My conscience made me feel worse than the spanking because I could see how punishing me put such a physical strain on her. I tried to make up for my bad behavior by doing little extra chores just to see her smile.

"Mutti," I told her, "When I get big I am going to be a doctor so I can make you feel better."

Immediately after they were married, my father had opened a tobacco shop. Eventually, with hard work, he succeeded in building up a thriving enterprise as a tobacco distributor. Years later, when I closed my eyes, I could still smell the sweetness of the tobacco and could picture the horseshoe shaped counter against the inside wall of my father's store.

He let me help him a little. "Get me the cigarettes over there in the small compartments on the right," he told me, and I scurried over feeling like a big helper. The center counter was where he greeted his customers and sold tobacco and pipes. When customers first came into the store, before they purchased tobacco, they headed to the left side of the store where he had his huge stamp collection. Word spread among his clients, and the collection attracted many interested customers. In the back of the shop were metal shelves where the supply of tobacco was stored.

I remember my father taking the tobacco, packing it into three by six inch boxes to be used in pipes, and delivering them to retailers. Soon the business expanded into selling wholesale as well as retail. I felt so grown up when I finally reached an age when I was able to make some of my father's deliveries on my scooter.

I think I was about five years old when my father sent me to the bank to make a deposit. On my way I stopped to look in a couple of store windows displaying wonderful mechanical toys. When I arrived at the bank, I realized I was short a few marks. Knowing my father's reaction when I did something wrong, I knew I would have to pay the dreadful consequences. I felt awful and when I got back to the store I told him, "Papa, I am so sorry, but I think I lost one or two marks."

He was furious. He screamed at me as he grabbed me by my arm. He pulled up my short pant leg and beat me severely with his hand saying, "Maybe this will teach you to be more careful with someone else's money."

Eventually, my father started to make enough money allowing us to have a full-time maid, Charlotte. She did most of the cooking, and also cared for my mother and me. I grew very fond of her.

Occasionally, my mother was well enough to visit her parents. "Come, shall we go to Alt Glienicke to visit Grossmutter and Grossvater?"

"Oh, yes, please. I love riding the train."

As on my father's first visit, we had to take a commuter train from Berlin to Mutti's village, and then transfer to a bus.

Mutti and I visited my grandparents on Christmas Eve. My father chose not to join us. I close my eyes today, and I can still feel the heat and see the huge coal burning stove decorated with colored tile. It was set in a corner of their living room. Its giant black pipe, always hot, climbed up to the ceiling. It fascinated me, and my grandmother knew it, so she made up stories about it.

Naturally, they had a Christmas tree. My cousins and I waited impatiently until Christmas Eve when the expected toys and sweets were distributed, after which mother and I returned home. It was a happy time for me because my mother was well enough to travel, and her family was so nice.

Shortly before mother's health started to rapidly deteriorate once again, Ewald asked my father, now a popular and successfully established tobacco merchant, to guarantee a loan for him.

"Arthur, do not do this thing," my mother insisted. "It is not wise for relatives to get involved with each other's money matters."

"But your brother is now my brother, and I feel…how can I say this…a certain loyalty to my adopted relatives. How can I not answer his request? He's our brother."

He did not take my mother's advise.

Chapter Three

I remember how I loved visiting my grandparents in the summer, especially since my father gave them one of our German shepherd dogs

We had two wonderful German Shepherd dogs, and once these dogs actually protected me from harm. The dogs had been trained to go out by themselves and return in thirty minutes, without being told.

We children who lived in the apartment building often used to play in the back of the house in a big, stone archway. It had a door through which deliveries were made. One day I was playing there alone, and a stranger approached me, pushed me into a corner and unbuttoned my pants. I trembled with terror.

"Keep your mouth shut and do not cry out, or I will hurt you."

I started to shake even more, but I did keep quiet and did as he told me since my father brought me up to always obey my elders. Just when this man was about to violate me, the dogs came trotting back. They must have sensed my fright, and they chased off the would be criminal and saved me.

I loved those dogs and enjoyed feeding them by hand. One night when my father arrived home from work, he saw what appeared to be my arm halfway down one of the dog's throat. Then and there, he decided the dogs had grown too dangerous to be around a small child.

He gave one away to strangers, and the other he gave to my grandparents. During my first few summers, when I visited Alt Glienicke, I always looked forward to playing with the dog.

In 1931, when I was six years old, my mother took a turn for the worse. Her family came to visit and tried to comfort her. Mother was very concerned about me. I listened while she told my grandparents, "I will feel better if you promise to be kind to the two men in my life while I am getting better."

I felt very grown up when I heard her refer to me as one of the two men in her life.

I guess she never really believed she would die...even when they took her to the hospital.

My father and I were in working in the back of his tobacco store when the telephone rang. It was a call from the hospital telling him my mother had just died.

"She's gone, my son." With a sob he told me, "Your mother is dead."

We sat down together on a wooden box, hugged each other and cried.

"Hanusch," my father said, calling me the pet name he had given me, "We are all alone now."

The funeral service was held in the cemetery chapel. I do not know how realistic my memories are, but it seemed my mother's body appeared to be propped up at a 45 degree angle in the open casket. I recall to this day how everyone sat in a semicircle around the coffin during the service. When the grave had been closed, in my childlike mind, the mound of dirt on top made it look to me almost like the casket was standing on top of the ground.

It is not a very happy memory.

Three months after my mother's death, her brother defaulted on the loan he had asked my father to guarantee. It was then I lost my childhood, sitting on the window sill of our apartment, watching the movers remove every piece of furniture to satisfy what became my father's obligation. The once cozy rooms were now bare. Only our personal belongings remained.

I knew my father needed me, but I didn't know how to help him or myself. "I'm not afraid, papa," I lied. "I just do not know what to do."

"We will be all right, Hanusch. We have each other."

I don't know if my uncle ever apologized to my father, but from that time on, I do not remember ever seeing him again. For the next year, my father and I lived in a furnished room, and with the help of my beloved Charlotte, the woman my father hired to run our household, I maintained some warmth and continuity in my life.

Now, with the new German laws making it more difficult for Jews to earn a living, my father had to do something to cut expenses. One morning, over breakfast, my father told me, "Hanusch, business is bad, and I'm afraid we can no longer afford to pay Charlotte her wages. I had to let her go."

"No, no, you cannot. I love Charlotte." I got up from the breakfast time and screamed defiantly stamping my foot. "I want Charlotte. I don't care what you say."

"Charlotte has been put in a sack and dropped into the River Spree," he snapped at me. And to add emphasis to her departure, he then told me, "Get dressed. I want to show you something."

Sniffling and crying, I managed to dress, and he took my hand and practically dragged me to a place on the bank of the river.

"This is where she was thrown in, and you will never see her again."

I was convinced.

Shortly after losing my Charlotte, another day came along, which would change my life drastically. Aware of the political climate now heating up in Germany, my father realized it was growing more dangerous for Jews even to walk in the streets.

He sat me down, and in a somber tone said, "Hanusch, do you remember how I told you about where I grew up?"

I could feel my lower lip tremble.

"You are a good boy," my father told me, "and I am not doing this to punish you, Hanusch, but it has become apparent to me it is not right to leave you unsupervised all day, especially in this political climate. So, for your own good, I have decided to send you to

Auerbach Orphanage."

"But papa, you said we will be all right because we have each other."

He continued, "This is not open for discussion. I am familiar with the place, and I feel sure you will receive proper care and supervision needed for an active, healthy six-year-old like you."

When people learn about my childhood, they say my father was an abusive parent. Perhaps it is true, but I believe the way I was raised probably saved my life.

I realized I was now in an unpleasant, troublesome situation from which escape seemed impossible.

And so, I was taken to the place where my father had grown up and learned how to be unfeeling, unmerciful and unrelenting.

Chapter Four

"Do you see that area over there? That's the center core of this place. It separates the girls and boys quarters," Arthur told his son, pointing to the middle of the great hall. And over there is the administration offices and the infirmary. I remember it as if it were yesterday."

The melancholy environment of the orphanage had not changed since it was built as a brewery in the late 1800s. Currently, it housed about one hundred children, some of whom were placed there, as Stephan was, by a single parent.

Stephan looked around at the gloomy L-shaped interior of the hallway while his father went to sign the necessary papers making his son an official resident. His heart began to beat faster, and he started hyperventilating making him feel light headed. His face paled.

When it was time for Arthur to leave, he bent down and hugged his son. Then, feeling slightly awkward, he pushed him away and shook hands with the six-year-old.

The young boy, numb, wide-eyed and afraid, was left standing alone in the foyer, clutching his small suitcase. His body rigid, his skin clammy, he had the miserable sensation of feeling completely abandoned and helpless. He did not know what to do. He fought back the tears. His father would not approve of tears. Finally, one of the older boys came along. "You must be the new one," he said. "My name is Peter. Come, I'll show you where to put your belongings. Then we'll go to the supervisor's office, and I'll introduce you."

Sighing, "the new one," as he was called, followed his guide silently to the sleeping quarters where he stowed away the few possessions he had brought with him. As he walked down a long, chilly corridor toward the office, he shivered. He couldn't tell whether it was from cold or fright…or maybe both.

"And who do we have here?" the grim looking man behind the desk asked.

"My name is Heinz Stephan Lewy."

"Heinz, eh? Well, we have too many boys here by that name, so from now on, you will be called by your middle name. Welcome to Auerbach, Stephan Lewy."

Stephan felt his identification had been ripped from him, and he had no option but to accept the situation.

The first night in the dormitory, Stephan quietly sobbed, burying his face into his pillow so no one would hear him. In the morning, abruptly awakened by a loud clanging bell, he found his pillow soaked with his tears.

It seemed the conditions in the orphanage and expectations of the children who lived there were similar to those in his father's house, so he knew what to expect. Nothing had changed, yet everything had changed. Stephen was not a spoiled child. His strict upbringing, and the lack of visible affection from his father, helped him fight his feelings of abandonment. Nothing was new, except from that time on, he acknowledged to himself that he really didn't have a father, just a relative who visited every Sunday.

The cold stone floor of the dormitory added to the room's spartan appearance. Standing between two steam covered, often frosted windows stood an old fashioned metal radiator which failed to heat not much more than the space in which it stood. The teachers' rooms between the dorms were arranged to prevent the students from engaging in an altercation at night without being caught.

"Come on, get those bodies out of bed. Everyone up. Hurry and get in line," the counselor's voice boomed as he clanged the bell.

Stephan barely had rubbed the sleep from his eyes when he was commanded to "Line up. Quickly."

The boys formed a line outside the single toilet facility shivering with cold. The washroom, with a marble slab about eighteen feet long, contained removable washbowls.

The instructor warned, "Use only the bowl assigned to you."

The next order came almost immediately. "When you are through washing yourselves, clean your wash basins, and polish the brass faucets," one of the older boys ordered.

"Get dressed, then make your bed. We don't have all day."

After he used the facilities and made his bed, Stephen looked for clean clothes. He was promptly told, "We change our clothes for clean ones once a week unless they are torn. Then we turn them over to the girls who repair them."

Confused, Stephan did his best to follow the instructions as he was taught at home, without question.

That night, in what was to be his weekly bath, he was sitting very comfortably in the bathtub, enjoying the warmth of the water, when another boy climbed in with him.

"Hey! What are you doing?" Stephan was mortified at the unexpected intrusion.

"Oh, you are the new one. Well, we sit two in a tub so we don't waste the water," his bathing companion explained. "Hurry up and wash," the experienced boy yelled at him. "We have to clean the tub and refill it for the next boys. When we dry off we have our body's inspected."

On his second morning in the orphanage someone said, "You, the new one," pointing to Stephan, "You are assigned to set the breakfast table and bring the food. When we are through, clear the dirty plates and put them on the dumbwaiter."

"But...but where?" said Stephan, his voice shaking, not wanting to ask, but needing to know.

"Just follow me," he was instructed.

And so he learned where to get the food and where the dumbwaiter was located.

After breakfast, the people in charge of the tables put together the standard type of school lunches which Stephan was to eat every day for the next several years.

"Is this all we get?" he asked the boy sitting next to him at the school lunch table as they opened their metal lunch boxes shaped like a loaf of bread.

"That's all there is," the boy told Stephen as he took out the four slices of bread with some butter scraped onto them. "Nothing more. An be sure and save the wrapper."

The bread, wrapped into one piece of waxed paper, had to be salvaged and returned to be used again for a full week. In the evening, as part of the main meal, they were served stews of pears or apples accompanied with rice. Generally, Stephan was grateful he found the food fairly edible although not appealing to the eye.

"Ugh, what is this with all the lumps in it?" he whispered to the boy seated next to him on the first time he was served an unfamiliar looking meal.

"That's beef stew with chunks of potato. You'll get no more, so if you don't want to feel hungry, you better eat it."

"Yeah, wait till you taste the sour herring they serve sometimes. They must keep it in buckets of sour juice just to give it a horrible taste."

"Tell you what we do," said another, in an undertone. "When we know we are having the herring, we smuggle in pieces of newspaper, and when no one is looking, we wrap the fish in the newspaper and drop it into the back side of the upright piano by the door as we march out."

"No one knows who does it, so no one gets punished."

Stephan was given a new assignment. He now was one of three boys in charge of polishing the shoes every night before going to bed. They always had two pairs, and it was mandatory they change shoes every day. This habit remained with Stephan for the rest of his life.

His father's strictness helped him cope with the tyrannical, uncompromising rules by which the orphanage was run. The children got their wallops and their punishments. If a child did something wrong, a teacher slapped him across his face or on the backs of his finger tips. Prohibiting Sunday visits, if a rule was broken, was the worst penalty of all.

Because Stephan was brought up in the same familiar authoritarian fashion, he actually believed this sort of punishment was nothing unusual. He also realized where his father had learned how to discipline.

Such was his existence in Auerbach.

Chapter Five

In spite of living in the severity of his new home, he started to feel less restricted out from under the eyes of his father's stern gaze, and was even willing to take some risks. Sometimes he rode in the dumbwaiter full of dirty dishes down to the kitchen.

"Wanna see something interesting?" he asked some of the boys. "Come with me," and he took them to a room his father had told him about with a warning "Never do what I did."

"My father did this when he used to live here. See, these air shafts? They are not used anymore, so we can climb into them and spy on the girls while they take their showers. My father said the best time to do it is when the older girls are there."

The boys had a good time looking. They tried to hold back their laughter, and when they were discovered, they laughed hysterically. In their victims' confusion, the embarrassed girls covered their faces with towels, causing side splitting hilarity among all the onlookers.

"Look, I bet they think covering their faces makes 'em invisible!"

They could hardly get out of the air shafts they were laughing so hard.

"Some of those girls are really built."

"Yeah, really built," Stephan acknowledged, even if he didn't know to what he was agreeing.

The boys all had a good time, but dared not do it again for months. Strangely, the girls never reported them.

Stephan was gaining a new perspective about his father now that he was being brought up in the same environment of rigidity and regulations. After all, his father received little or no tenderness or compassion in his youth, and no nurturing role model since he lost his family at such an unusually young age.

"As an adult, I never held my father's methods against him, although I felt the punishments I had to endure were too harsh and unreasonably strict.

"He corrected me continually because he was a perfectionist, and wanted me to be perfect," he once told a friend. "Maybe what he did was right—at least it was all he knew how to do."

Although Stephan was afraid of him, he never ever doubted his father's love. He was grateful, however, as a young child, he had experienced affection, gentleness and kindness from his mother.

The religious observances in the orphanage were not the really strict narrow practice of the orthodox, although the dietary laws, based on health, were strictly observed. This included keeping dairy meals separate from meat dishes by six hours.

The older boys were compelled to attend services in the chapel three times a day located in the synagogue upstairs. On Friday evening and Saturday morning, attendance was compulsory. The synagogue was also used by the Jewish families in the area.

On Friday night, before the Sabbath meal, the candles were lighted, a prayer was said prior to the pouring the wine and eating the bread, and then again after finishing the meal.

Although many of the sacred religious holy days were ignored, at Passover there was a special Seder meal, and unlike most meals, this one included the girls who also lived in the orphanage. The tables were set formally, and the entire Passover story was read.

At Chanukah, they lighted candles, one added every evening for each of the eight days, and every child received a small gift from the people running the orphanage.

Every boy learned to conduct services. They had so many classes in Hebrew they all could read it fluently. Upon turning thirteen, the boys took turns saying the prayers after the Friday evening Sabbath meal. On Saturday evening, a special braided candle was used in a simple ritual to usher out the Sabbath.

Stephan was totally surrounded by his religion and lived Judaism more than he ever did at home.

Chapter Six

"Heinrich, your shoes were not properly polished; therefore, your Sunday visiting hours are canceled."

"Erich, your shirt was hanging out of your pants. No Sunday visit for you."

The orders came down from the orphanage administrators. Any infraction of the rules the officials did not hesitate to restrict us from visiting our family.

And so it went.

Although I had lots of acquaintances, I don't remember making many close friends at the orphanage. I guess we were too preoccupied trying to do well and avoid punishment, rather than focus on individual friendships.

Occasionally, we got together for fun. We had a courtyard where we boys played soccer. We also played chess and hit a tennis ball off a brick wall. For the younger children there was a king-sized sandbox.

A big infraction in the orphanage was being discovered reading another book we sneaked inside our big prayer book. We had to be very careful not to get caught.

"You sure looked like you were into the services last night," my friend Josef told me. "Were you smuggling in a different book for a change?"

"What of it," I answered trying not to admit to my crime.

I had been reading my favorite detective story, Emil and the Detectives. The book was about the size of the current issues of Reader's Digest, just the right dimensions to conceal in the prayer book. When I attended services, I used to disguise the forbidden book with a cover to make it look as if it might actually be a prayer book.

"I know you were. Can I borrow it when you get finished?" Josef asked.

"Well, okay, but just don't call attention to me in the service. I have to be very careful because I know if they catch me doing something I shouldn't, my father will probably give me a smack along with the punishment I will get from the rabbi.

I had been in the orphanage about a year when I was called into the superintendent's office. "I am sorry to tell you," the man said abruptly, with no explanation, "you will not be allowed to go home for a Sunday visit until further notice."

My seven-year-old mind raced back over the week. I could barely catch my breath. Devastated, I whimpered, biting my lip, failing to prevent the tears spilling over my face. "But...but what did I do?" I never imagined I had ever been so bad as to be treated this way.

"You have done nothing wrong. The request has come from your father."

Frustrated, frightened and furious, I did not know where to direct my rage. I ground my teeth until my jaws ached. What is going to happen to me. I was being abandoned. Now my terror turned to hate toward the person responsible for this—my own father.

In the orphanage the older boys talked of nothing else but the news in all the papers about official new laws now being enforced.

"Now the new government is banning Jews from holding public office," Fritz, a tall lanky blonde from Weim told us.

"Yes, also from civil service positions, newspaper jobs, farming, teaching, radio and theater arts. There soon will be nothing left," his friend Arnie added.

About the same time these laws were being implemented, I received special permission to visit one of my uncles, my late mother's youngest brother, Ewald. This would be the first time I heard from him since we lost everything when he defaulted. However, my feelings soared. At least my mother's family was not abandoning me. I was pleased to escape from the dreary routine of the weekends in the orphanage.

I was told, "We will pick you up after your dinner, around eight o'clock."

It wasn't a pleasant visit. My disagreeable aunt smacked me because she said I got the towel dirty after washing my hands.

"I hope you will appreciate what we went through to get you here. We had to pick you up after dark because we did not want you to be seen by our neighbors. The new laws could get us into great trouble," my uncle told me.

It was the first and last time I was invited. After that visit I never saw either of them again.

My grandmother visited me once or twice but never in the orphanage. I was picked up around the corner. She did not want to be seen entering a Jewish orphanage.

Political pressures were increasing for Jews. By now, April 1, 1933, signs on business windows screamed at passers by, "Don't Buy From Jews." I knew my father was a devout Socialist, and even though I felt bitterness toward him for abandoning me, I still was concerned about his safety. I was afraid he would be seriously affected by all this.

I had no explanation for months of why my father deserted me. Finally, I learned he had been arrested and put into Oranienburg, a concentration camp located near Berlin, then primarily a work and detention camp.

When I found out, I asked the director of the orphanage, "Why didn't you tell me in the first place? I am eight years old. I would have understood."

"Well, we thought you would be less scared if you didn't know where he was."

Now, I felt really angry. "When will they let him out so he can take me home?" I was ready to kill the messenger.

He was imprisoned there for about a year. During his incarceration, he was severely beaten, his teeth were knocked out, and he experienced his first heart attack. Eventually, he was discharged a broken man.

At last he came to see me once he was released. I was shocked into silence when I saw him. My anger disappeared. I hardly recognized his poor tortured face. Then, when I put my arms around his emaciated body, and he hugged me back, I melted. I knew he was different, softer, I think.

I too had changed. That year lots of things changed. As Chancellor of Germany, Hitler suspended freedom of speech, freedom of assembly and freedom of the press. During the year I didn't see my father, I became so efficiently mischievous I rarely was caught, and at the age of twelve was rewarded for such good behavior by being given certain privileges.

From a religious standpoint, I wasn't supposed to prepare the Torah portion—the first five books of the Hebrew Scriptures—until I had turned thirteen and had been bar mitzvah—a rite of passage for boys. However, I was given the responsibility and the honor of opening the synagogue in the morning. I reset the Torah scrolls for the day's reading, and I turned on the electric organ to warm it up.

As for academia, we didn't receive what could be called a model education. It was nothing one could call typical. Until 1934, I went to regular public school with children of all religions. We had a forty minute walk to get there, so we left the orphanage around 7:30 and arrived at school by 8:30 or 9:00.

We Jewish children were now vividly aware of the existing anti-Semitism everywhere in our lives. It seems we could no longer escape it or be protected from it.

"Lets take this shortcut," someone suggested. "Maybe we can avoid those damned Nazi Schweine Hunds who look to beat us up."

"Stay together," someone else suggested. "And don't let them hear you swear at them."

So we walked in small groups for what safety and protection we hoped it would give us. However, our method rarely was successful. We were often beaten up and incapable of doing anything about it. We figured this was just part of our schooling. It was a pretty scary existence. If the police were present, they just stood around and watched us get walloped.

In the school, things were not much better. If we Jewish boys did not conform to what the teachers required, or if we made more than five mistakes on a spelling test, or if we scored below a certain grade in handwriting, the teacher lifted the legs of our short pants and beat us mercilessly with a flexible stick until we nearly lost consciousness. Furthermore, if we talked when we weren't supposed to, or if we didn't do immediately what we were told, we were smacked across the knuckles with a ruler.

Most of the time, to my teachers' disappointment, I was able to avoid beatings since my favorite subjects were spelling and math, which called for definite answers, not opinions.

Chapter Seven

In the years between 1934 and 1935, the early days of Nazism, a group known as "the Brown Shirts," a gang of hooligans who upheld Nazi ideology, was going around harassing people who didn't fit their idea of a "proper Aryan." Even adults weren't spared humiliation. One Sunday my father, who had by now gained back most of his strength, had picked me up at Auerbach, and we were headed for my favorite sweet shop. As we walked together talking about nothing in particular, one of his garters, the type men used in those days to hold up their stockings, became undone, and his sock drooped just below his pant cuff.

A Nazi goon snapped at my father, spitting out the words like bullets, in a loud voice so everyone around could hear, "Hey…Jew boy. Your garter belt is down."

In anger my father pulled his eight inch long, white metal house key out of his pocket and smacked the "Brown Shirt" on the face with it. He then grabbed my hand and pulled me with him, racing breathlessly down the street, ducking into the first doorway we came to, successfully avoiding further "discussion."

Fear made me sweat. Running made me breathless. "Why did you do that, Papa? We could have been beaten up, even killed!"

"I have taken enough crap from those brown shirted bastards. That is why I did it…and it felt good."

Patterns of confrontation were common for my father. As a Socialist, he was constantly putting himself in a position of having to defend himself. One year later, this type of incident would have surely cost us our lives. As it was, we were lucky to get away without enduring bodily harm.

The Nazi net was tightening, strangling everyone caught in its web. By 1935 the German policy makers in the Nazi party decided their next step was to "purify" their race by killing the mentally retarded and separating people they considered inferior. That included all Jews.

A Nazi officer addressed our class. "We do not want Jews to adulterate our pure Aryan race by associating with us, so from now on, all Jews will be required to attend schools exclusively reserved for them. You are to leave this school immediately."

We were puzzled, but we didn't question. We all got up, collected our things and filed out in an orderly fashion. When we returned to the orphanage, the people in charge had already been informed of the edict. A school was soon set aside for us in a building about a half hour away.

Children as well as adults can be cruel, and Jewish children are no exception. Even in the Jewish school, we had a social strata. Among our class of fifty-two students, we made it a point to find out who was of German descent.

"What kind of a name is Koski?" someone asked a classmate.

"I don't know...German, I think," the boy answered nervously.

"Doesn't sound German to me," another boy said.

Then we quickly decided to prove we were superior to students who were of a different background by beating them up. In our ignorance we did not recognize the similar characteristics we were displaying to those who were persecuting us. Certainly, no distinction was made by the Hitler Youth. This was an organization of boys, mobilized into the National Socialist community, to prepare them for combat. And they practiced on us.

Walking back to the orphanage was almost like treading through a mine field. It made my skin prickle with apprehension.

"I wonder how many of us will be able to avoid being beaten up by the those rotten thugs who come looking for someone to use like a football."

"They are probably waiting for us right now outside the Jewish school," Paul answered me.

"Oh Jesus," I said when saw those uniformed hoodlums. "They

are making a gauntlet."

"God," Robby swore. "They are taking off their belts."

"I hope their Scheisse pants fall down."

We all giggled with nervousness as we met the foe.

We ran through their line, and they whipped us with the buckle ends of their belts. Once again the police stood by and did nothing. I could hear the screams when the buckles hit. For the Hitler Youth, this was part of their training program. Me? I just ran like hell.

One day when I was around ten and about to be graduated from grade school, my teacher approached me saying, "I'd like you to come over to my house Saturday. I have some advise I want to talk to you about."

This was quite an honor to be invited to an instructor's house while he strung his "pearls of wisdom." I was flattered.

This instructor must have enjoyed the influence he had over us young boys. So every Saturday afternoon I went to his house. He would sit me on his lap while he was talking, and eventually I would feel his hand find its way up my short pant leg. I squirmed. I didn't know what he was doing, but I didn't want to be disrespectful.

"I don't think it is necessary for you to go to high school. I think you would be better off finding a job in which you earned money. You would like that, wouldn't you—to have enough money in your pocket to buy what you wanted?"

He got permission for me to take the job he told me about.

"It's a good job, as a cook in the Jewish hospital," he said.

He didn't mention the hospital had two very orthodox kosher kitchens which used separate utensils for meat from those used for milk products.

I was told, "Your job will be to peel potatoes and carrots. When you are through doing that, wash the floors."

One day I had a question to ask and walked across the archway from the kitchen used for cooking meat dishes to the one used for handling milk recipes. I had a knife in my hand. I didn't touch a thing, but before I could ask my question there was an uproar.

"You contaminated the knife," the man screamed at me.

"But what did I do? What did I do? I didn't touch anything!" I screamed back.

"The knife must be purified and stuck into the ground for 24 hours!" His face turned purple with rage.

Their words were law. I took off my apron, and went downstairs, knife in hand. Suddenly, the hairs on the back of my neck stood at attention when I realized I was walking between marble slabs on which rested several dead bodies waiting for burial. A man, I think they called a watcher, or a minder, was sitting in a stall shaped like a telephone booth located in the center of this room, presumably praying for the dead. My stomach churned, and my mouth filled with saliva. I was ill prepared for the sight and overwrought by the experience.

I ran outside where there was a small area of soil in the back, and stuck the knife into the ground with a vengeance. The next morning I quit my job, and I have never cooked since.

While I remained fairly healthy most of the time, when I did get sick, it was rather serious.

"I'm afraid you have a severe case of diphtheria, my boy," the doctor told me, "and you will have to be taken to the hospital in an ambulance."

Memories came flooding back. I could barely talk, my throat was so swollen. I could feel my heart thumping, thumping, thumping.

"I don't want to go to the hospital. Please, I don't want to go." Croaking my plea with all my strength, all I could think of was "Mutti went in an ambulance, and she died in the hospital."

Fortunately, no one listened to my protests, and when I was admitted, I remained totally isolated behind four glass walls until the prescribed medication took effect. One of my father's friends visited and brought me a present…pampelmus, a grapefruit. It was most unusual and rare to have tropical fruits in Germany in those days, so to me it seemed like a treasure. The only tropical foods I remember in Germany were oranges from the Middle East and bananas from North Africa.

Chapter Eight

Fully recovered, Stephan was able to return to the orphanage. The Nazis continued to affect his very existence. The Nuremberg Laws now went into effect adding more complications to his young life. Jews were now deprived of their German citizenship; they were diminished to the status of "subjects," eliminating a large part of the population's civil rights.

"Listen to what those Fascist pigs are doing to us," Arthur read to his son from the newspaper while on their Sunday visit. "We are not allowed to marry non-Jews. Maybe it is a good thing your mother is gone." He paused and shook his head in disbelief. "And we cannot employ female Aryan servants under the age of thirty-five years old. This will get worse. Mark my words."

Stephan knew times were bad, but as a ten-year-old he couldn't grasp the absolute seriousness of the situation.

Arthur's prediction were to germinate and sprout as weeds do in a carpet of grass.

Momentarily there was a respite from the worst of the persecution. Joseph Goebbels, Minister of Propaganda, convinced a reluctant Hitler of the propaganda value if Germany hosted the winter and summer Olympic games in 1936. In February, Germany hosted the Winter Olympics at Garmisch-Partenkirchen in the Bavarian Alps. Western journalists observed troop maneuvers at Garmisch and reported it to their editors. During the summer Olympics, the Nazis decided to disguise the military presence.

Signs stating "Jews not wanted" and similar anti-Jewish slogans were removed. Jews were given many of the same privileges non-Jews had.

"Look Papa," Stephen said to his father as they walked down

Kurfürstendamm, one of the well known streets running through Berlin. "The signs are down. We can sit on the benches and walk in the park. Maybe you were wrong. Maybe things are really getting better."

"It won't last. This is all political propaganda. Mark my words," he told his naive son.

For the time being, the German press, radio, publishers and film were censored, admonishing them not to say anything that might upset the Olympic visitors.

Discreetly, during the festivities, Sachsenhausen Concentration Camp was being built just 18 miles north of Berlin. In September of 1936, political opponents of the regime—liberals, socialists, as well as Jehovah Witnesses and homosexuals were being incarcerated there.

The Olympics were a huge success for Germany, in spite of the many medals won by African Americans. By the time the Olympics ended, Hitler's popularity created a juggernaut so powerful the German people followed him blindly, and with deep devotion, into what eventually would lead them into the abyss of hell. Their depraved allegiance was so great and destructive the Germans were willing to follow him to their deaths—which many of them did. Nothing could stop him.

Twelve days after the Winter Olympics and five months before the Summer Games, German troops crossed the Rhine River and penetrated the demilitarized zone between Germany and France.

After the Olympics, when the Nazis were certain it would no longer hurt their international image, civil rights were once again taken away from the Jewish citizens of Germany.

"Well, my smart young son, you thought maybe your papa was wrong, eh? Maybe things are really getting better? Well, now you see. We are once again excluded from sitting on public benches and using the parks. See those signs? They prohibit us from using public transportation. We cannot even run our own businesses anymore."

"My God. In that case at least half the Jewish population has no way of earning a living."

"You always were good with figures," his father said with a smirk. "Unfortunately, this new law creates a huge predicament. I'm afraid I will have to sell my store," Arthur told his son. "People are taking advantage of the situation, and the most anyone has offered me is 1,200 Reich Mark."

"That's not much, is it, Papa?"

"In America it would come to about $300. Not much indeed. I'm afraid I will have to accept the offer before Hitler decides to take it for free."

By this time Stephan had reached his eleventh birthday and felt as anxious and as powerless as his father. "What are we going to do for money?" he asked.

Desperate, Arthur had to find a way to earn a living for himself and for his financial obligations to the orphanage. Fortunately, with help he found a way to covertly remove some of his supplies before the new owner took possession.

Knowing he had to do something, Arthur started a dangerous arrangement of illegally replenishing tobacco, cigarettes and pipe supplies for cooperative retailers with whom he had previously done business. These businessmen were willing to take illicit risks because they liked and respected Arthur Lewy and wanted to help him.

He took Stephan into his confidence. "Just in case anything happens to me, you should know what I am doing. After dark, when stores are closed, I go to the retail shops and pick up orders hidden under a door mat."

"What do you do with the orders? You don't have the store anymore."

"That's why this is so complicated. I secretly deliver the goods I have on hand to friendly wholesalers. In turn they pay me a commission, and I can buy more from cooperative dealers."

For Stephan to remain in the orphanage seemed the most practical thing for all concerned, and so that is where he continued to live until July, 1939, visiting home on Sundays and some holidays.

Stephan's life was about to change. His shyness still kept him from making close friends easily, but he did become friendly with a boy named Gunther who would become very significant in Stephan's future. The two boys had a similar situation. Gunther's mother, Maria, a divorcee, had to work full time and wanted her son to have supervision.

One memorable Sunday, when she came to pick up her son at the orphanage, Maria noticed Stephan sitting by himself.

"Doesn't that little boy have anyone to take him out?"

"Yes," Gunther said. "He's waiting for his father."

"Why don't you ask him if he and his father would like to come home with us for coffee," she suggested to Gunther.

Gunther approached Stephan and tried to coax him to accept his mother's invitation.

"Thanks, but I am waiting for my father. He'll be here soon."

When Arthur arrived, Maria was still there and cordially encouraged the Lewys to join her at her apartment for coffee and cake.

"Can we, Papa? Can we?" Stephan asked, charmed by the mention of cake.

So, the four of them went to Maria's apartment and spent a pleasant afternoon. After the visit, the boys became slightly more friendly.

Once more, on another Sunday when Arthur came to get Stephan, he arrived at the same time as Maria. Again she graciously invited them to her home, and soon it started to be a regular event. The two adults seemed to like each other and had a great deal to talk about.

One Sunday, Maria invited her sister, Johanna, to join them. She couldn't possibly have known how this would affect all their lives.

Johanna smiled after the Lewys left. "Maria," she told her sister, "this man is not for you."

"How do you know that?"

"I know you, and I can see what kind of a person he is. You two would be like oil and water—you'd never mix. You'd probably kill each other."

Maria felt disappointed since she started to think of Arthur as a possible permanent arrangement, but she valued and respected her sister's opinion. She knew Johanna was right.

"You know, maybe you and he…"

"We'll see. Don't push anything," Johanna said.

After spending a few Sundays together, Maria could see how Arthur and Johanna were attracted to one another. Soon they started to see each other not only on Sundays but regularly at other times. One beautiful September day, in 1937, Arthur came to pick up twelve-year-old Stephan and brought Johanna along. The three of them walked to a Jewish owned Konditerei which oddly enough had been allowed to stay open. Here they served coffee, tea, milk and wonderful cream cakes, among other favorite sweets Stephan enjoyed.

"We have something to tell you, Hanusch," his father said with an unusual look of pleasure registering on his face.

"You like Johanna, don't you?"

"Sure I do. You're nice," Stephan answered looking at her before popping another cookie into his mouth.

"Thank you, Stephan," "Johanna said as she pushed a slice of almond cake covered with thick whipped cream onto his plate. He ate it in two gulps.

"Take your time, dear. Why do you eat so fast?" Johanna asked.

"At the orphanage, if we finish first, we can sometimes have seconds." Eating quickly is a habit he never broke. For the moment his hint was ignored.

"I'm glad you like her because…well, she and I have decided to get married. What do you think of that?"

"It's swell, Papa. Please may I have another piece of cake?"

And so, in 1938 Arthur and Johanna were married in a small ceremony with only her relatives attending. Stephan felt quite comfortable with this considerate, compassionate woman and started calling her "Mutti." She was very pleased at such devotion.

"I guess you and I are cousins now. I am really lucky to have a wonderful second mother," he told Gunther after the wedding reception.

"She's a great aunt, too," he answered.

Johanna showered a great deal of affection on the two new men in her life, which was probably the only positive thing that happened to Stephan in 1938. Otherwise, it was the worst year in his childhood.

Johanna worked full-time as a bookkeeper for the Cohn family when she came into Stephan's life. Sigmund Cohn's wife, Helen, had a brother, Ludwig Herzberg, who lived in Magdeburg, sixty miles west of Berlin. He and his son, Ernst, sometimes visited the office and were acquainted with Johanna. Years later, Ernst and his wife Lillian were to become an important part of Stephan's life.

Johanna's office was located conveniently close to Stephan's new school. Once a week, she left for the office a half hour earlier than usual, met Stephan at her subway station, and swapped sandwiches with him. So, for the next few months, he occasionally had a fairly decent lunch. It was his treat for the week, and he didn't advertise it to the others.

After Johanna and Arthur married, the only living accommodation available to them was his furnished room with a kitchen they shared with their landlady.

"I'm sorry this is all we can afford at the moment," Arthur apologized to his bride. The furnishings consisted of two beds, an old fashion marble top wash table, a desk, table and sofa where Stephan slept when he visited them. There was no bathtub, and they had to wash in a porcelain bowl.

"We'll be fine, Arthur…just fine."

Arthur realized he was lucky for a second time in his life.

Chapter Nine

Six months before I turned thirteen, I faced what seemed to me to be a crucial time in my life. It was when I started to learn the challenging and extremely important ritual necessary for the ceremony of bar mitzvah, celebrating the time when, as a Jewish boy, I would take responsibility for assisting in religious services. I was having great difficulty both with the necessary chanting, and with the cantor, a perfectionist, who was teaching me. I found it absolutely impossible to reach a certain note in the portion I had to sing.

"NO, no, no," the cantor screamed at me. "Stop and do it again," he said every time I came to this section. "I will have you repeat it until you do it right."

Or die, I thought.

This went on during the entire six month training period. Finally, on the last rehearsal before my bar mitzvah, the elusive note and I blended harmoniously. Needless to say, the cantor was as thrilled as I. And so, in March, two of my friends with birthdays close to my own, led the congregation of the orphanage and a few invited guests in prayer as part of the observance.

By this time, the laws denying civil liberties to German Jews had become more severe, restricting our income, limiting what work we were allowed to do, limiting for whom we could work.

A few days before my big event, my new mother explained, "Since the orphanage is limited as to what it can provide, I'm afraid it cannot cater any special food for our celebration. And I feel really sad we have to limit your party to only twelve people, but it is all we can afford. So, how would you like to have your favorite meal at home, like a party?"

"I'd like that."

Then she asked me, "What special food would you like?"

Without hesitation I answered, "Corn beef and cabbage will be a real treat!"

After the service, the ten or twelve family friends who arrived to hear me conduct the services came to my parents' apartment for the celebration dinner. My parents, my mother's two sisters, now my aunts, their mother, now my grandmother, Gunther, and a few of my father's friends, all came to celebrate my big day.

It was shortly after the noon hour when my father opened the front door with the same eight inch key he had used years ago in response to the thug who ridiculed him. As we all walked up the twelve steps to the apartment, I inhaled the wonderful aroma filling the hallway from the already prepared dinner conspicuously announcing my special request.

Then we noticed a tall, muscular, uniformed SS officer casually leaning against the wall at the top of the staircase. The sight of him sent a chill through us all.

In a extremely sharp, menacing tone, he demanded of my father, "What is your name?" and when he answered, he was arrested immediately, brutally shoved downstairs and hauled away.

The joyful atmosphere of the occasion changed to one of shock and apprehension. We all entered the apartment, and our guests stayed with us waiting—for what we did not know. No one could eat. Finally, around seven or eight o'clock, my father returned.

"Would you believe I was not really arrested?" Then sarcastically he added, "Would you also believe the officials just wanted to award me the Front Line Soldier's Medal for having fought for my country in World War I?"

"Oh yes. I believe you. I think I read somewhere Hitler had decreed all veterans of World War I be awarded that medal," a guest announced. "Makes me absolutely paranoid."

"How beautifully ironic. In 1933, I was thrown in prison by the German government, and now, in 1938, I am presented with an award for loyal war service from the same government who currently wants to kill me. It is a crazy and dangerous time."

He poured himself a drink and turned to me and started to preach in more than his usual rebuking, angry tone. In front of our guests, he lectured me on how to care for my mother when "I am no longer among the living."

I felt guilty and didn't know why. Then I heard my father make his terrible prediction. "I am suspicious of the general conditions in this country, including the magnanimous gesture of giving me this once considered honorable symbol. It makes me very nervous. More and more, it looks as if Germany will certainly go to war. If not this year, then surely next year, and early in September."

I asked, "But how can you be so sure of the month?"

His words were ominous. He put his hands on my shoulders, looked straight into my eyes and said, "If possible, Germany will always want to start a war after the wheat crop is in the barn, and in Germany, like clockwork, September 1st is the day to gather in the crop. On September 2nd there is enough wheat for the first winter of war, enough to feed one's army. And that is how I am sure. Now, lets eat!"

Since my father was always lecturing me about one thing or another, I had difficulty recognizing whether or not he was indeed blaming me for the entire political environment.

With a sense of dejection, I "celebrated" my bar mitzvah!

Chapter Ten

Stephan couldn't know, but even before they were married, his parents had started a process to help them all leave Germany. And after the Soldier's Medal incident, the reality of the current situation hit Arthur and Johanna quite forcefully.

"We have to do something and do it fast," Arthur told his wife. "I just found out if anyone has passage booked to anywhere out of Germany, that person will not be arrested and will be free to leave. That's one way of getting rid of us."

"I have a cousin, a very distant cousin in America," Johanna told Arthur. "I'll write her a letter…"

"Better send a cablegram," Arthur interrupted. "We don't have too much time."

The United States government required all potential immigrants to have an affidavit of support. This mandatory statement declared these people will not be a financial burden to the public once they arrived in America. It was essential to have a sponsor.

They received an answer to their cable almost immediately. "They say she and her family will be happy to sponsor us with an affidavit. Isn't that wonderful?"

"Thank God we have someone willing to do this for us."

"Yes, I know,"Johanna agreed. "I guess I'm pretty lucky to have a convenient second cousin."

"I am going to book passage right now on ships headed for Cuba, Shanghai and America. We do not have to pay anything until later, and this way we will be assured the possibility of being able to leave here. Whichever ship comes first will decide which place will be our destination."

"But what about affidavits?"

"Only the United States requires them."

"We shouldn't wait too long to apply then," she advised.

At breakfast, a few days later, Arthur read aloud to Johanna from ran article in the newspaper. "Well, it has started."

"What has started?" Johanna asked as she poured another cup of ersatz coffee.

"Starting tomorrow, meat, coffee and butter are to be rationed. I know what that means."

"What are you saying?"

"I am saying I am more certain than ever, war is imminent, especially since butter is being rationed."

"What about butter?"

"A byproduct of butter, my dear Johanna, is used as a lubricant for cannons."

"You cannot be serious."

"You watch."

That ended their breakfast.

It was Wednesday, November 9th. On his way home from school Stephan's eye caught the newspaper headlines from the kiosk on the corner. He bought a copy thinking he would have something to discuss with his father. He surmised from past conversations with him this headline meant more trouble for them as Jews, but he could never imagine just how much.

All over Germany, the influential arm of the newspapers, in big, bold, black headlines, incited the public with a tornado-like force, reaping its destructive motive.

JEW KILLS GERMAN ATTACHÉ.

JEW RESPONSIBLE FOR MURDERING GERMAN ATTACHÉ.

"They are advising Jewish men over a certain age to turn themselves in. Right now they have us where they want us," Arthur said to Hannah when he read the newspaper. "Those National Socialists will use this distraught young man's motives as justification to blame Jews worldwide for every misfortunate occurrence going on in this country."

"What do you think they will do?" Johanna asked.

"Why, they will begin their plan for getting rid of the Jews—JUDEN FREI."

By now the streets had exploded with shrieking uniformed goons as well as hysterical civilians. "Get rid of the Jews." "Germany for the Germans."

Arthur worried about what more could happen…and about Stephan's safety. Sneaking down the dark back streets, attempting to avoid the screaming and frenzied public in the streets, he managed to make his way to the orphanage.

"Those Nazi bastards are preparing for something horrible. They are dragging Jewish men right out of their homes and arresting them right and left," Arthur told the orphanage supervisors when he arrived to check on Stephan. "Stay inside everyone," he advised before leaving.

Believing Stephan was safe at Auerbach, Arthur went into hiding to avoid being taken prisoner. Later, Stephan learned a few of his friends were taken hostage until their fathers turned themselves in.

Later that evening, the events reaped the whirlwind, and all hell broke loose.

"Looks like there's a big fire. Let's go see," Gunther said, looking out the window.

"We're not supposed to leave," Stephan answered.

"Well, I'm going. Come along if you aren't afraid."

The challenge worked. The two boys sauntered down the street edging their way toward the red glow. Soon sounds of loud terrifying screams mixed with the noise of clanging fire bells and crashing glass made the boys shiver with fright.

"Don't go so fast, Gunther. They'll see us."

"Stay close," Gunther hissed.

The boys hugged the side of a building to make it more difficult to be seen. What they saw made them freeze in their tracks.

"Look, the synagogue is on fire, and the firemen are letting it burn. And the Nazis are beating some men right in the street. And the people standing around are jeering, those bastards."

"They are letting it burn. They are only trying to save the buildings next to it. Oh, my God."

"Jesus, those goons are smashing the windows of the stores marked with the star of David. There's broken glass all over the place. We better get out of here," Gunther yelled over the din.

"Yes, lets get out of here," Stephan agreed.

This was "Kristallnacht," the Night of the Broken Glass.

They hurried back to the orphanage just in time to be caught in a roundup of its inhabitants by black uniformed Nazis.

"Everyone next door, into the synagogue. Hurry up, you Jew bastards."

The synagogue at the orphanage which served the children and surrounding Jewish community was not set on fire. Instead, the Nazis pushed and shoved the one hundred children and their teachers into the building.

"What's happening?" some of the younger children asked.

The Nazis left after cutting the gas line which provided the flame for the eternal light. The gas started to seep into the room full of children.

Stephan recognized the sound of the door being bolted from the outside. The younger children started to cough and to cry.

"I'm scared," one of the younger boys said.

"What's happening?" another asked.

"What should we do," they questioned each other."

Someone pointed out, "What if we try to get out? Maybe they will shoot us."

In a flash Stephan said, "Either way, if we stay here we'll die."

Just then one of the older boys took a chair and hurled it through a stain glass window allowing the fumes to escape and saving the lives of those locked inside.

A neighbor, who secretly watched out her window to what was happening, came and unbolted the door, and the children poured out of the room, coughing, crying and very frightened. The parents who had children in the orphanage could not check on their safety since going outdoors might have meant death.

"Stay inside," the caretakers warned the children. "The Nazi goons are beating and arresting any Jew from sixteen to sixty they can find."

This announcement made Stephan very concerned about his father. He thought he might go into hiding, but would he get caught?

He knew his parents had made contingency plans for such an occasion. The Jewish population continued to be at the mercy of the Nazis. The Gestapo persisted in arresting Jews at random, on any pretext or no justification at all.

Meanwhile, very early the next morning, Johanna was awakened by the dreaded sound of banging on the door. Two uniformed officers yelled. "Gestapo. Open up. Open up now."

When she got up, put on her robe and opened the door, the taller of the two men yelled in her face, "Where is your husband?"

"I do not know. I assume he went to work."

"Who else is here? Where are your children?"

"We have no children. We are recently married."

Johanna knew if the man of the house was not found, his child would be taken as hostage. And the Nazis knew a father would turn himself in to free his child. In this case, since no child was available as hostage, the Gestapo sat around waiting for Arthur's return.

Johanna nervously asked permission to go to the bathroom remembering the contingency plans she and Arthur had created to avoid such an arrest.

"As long as I am up, may I take the cover off our parrot's cage so he can get some light?"

"Hurry up. Just do it."

Johanna removed the cover and moved the cage into the window. Arthur had made it a point many times to leave home about three o'clock in the morning to avoid the Gestapo's usual early morning four o'clock arrivals, often used as a frightening ploy.

"Ach," Arthur said to himself when he returned home, and looked up to see if the cage was visible. "I'll have to disappear for another 24 hours. Poor Johanna to be put through this on my account." And he stole away to hide for another day.

That morning Stephan and his friends, Henry and Gunther, surveyed the damage on their way to school.

"I can't believe what they did," Stephan said to Henry when he saw the desecration, Prayer shawls and Torah scrolls had been trampled on as they lay in the streets.

"They must be insane," Henry said.

"Jesus…look…some of those goons are still looting. We better get out of here," Stephan whispered.

Gunther and Henry agreed.

The next day, Thursday, the boys were instructed to pick up their lunches and walk to the Jewish school. "After all," their supervisors told them, "life goes on."

And so Stephan and the rest of the students did what they did every day. They picked up their lunches and walked to the Jewish school. What they saw sickened them. Jewish men were still being beaten and humiliated while forced to sweep the streets. What Stephan didn't know was that Jewish families were being forced to pay for the damages inflicted upon them by others.

When Stephan and his friends arrived at school, regular classes had been canceled. Instead, the teachers explained to their students what was happening.

"I'm afraid our country's Jewish citizens are being deprived of all we hold dear. We are being forced out of the universities, the medical and legal professions. It's a travesty."

When Stephan met with his parents on the following Sunday, he learned from his father what was behind the headlines he saw in the papers.

"A Polish Jew, living in Paris, shot the Nazi attaché at the German Embassy in retaliation over the murder of his parents by the Nazis in Poland," Arthur told his son.

"Hitler's henchmen claimed the rioting was spontaneous, but anyone in his right mind would know this destruction was organized, those bastards," Arthur said.

After Kristallnacht the Puls, Stephan's grandparents, two uncles and their families stopped all contact with him in order not to be seen associating with Jews. Hitler's power and influence had taken effect, and his mother's family didn't want to be affiliated with Jews or even be seen with one, and certainly didn't want to be related to one.

In the orphanage the children gathered in the room that served as an auditorium. The headmaster went to the podium in the front of the room, raised his hand to quiet the noisy boys, and started his announcement.

"We have received notice that all Jews will soon be required to carry identification cards stamped with a 'J.' All legal documents required for Jews will be stamped with the middle name of 'Israel' for the men, and 'Sarah' for the women. These items will be distributed to you as soon as they are available."

Chapter Eleven

"Today is the day we have an appointment for the physical examination at the American Consulate required by the United States government before they will issue us a visa," Arthur reminded Johanna. "If I get home before you, I'll start dinner," he said as he went out the door.

Johanna got home first and was nearly through preparing their meal when Arthur finally arrived. Johanna saw by the expression on his face he felt despondent.

"They say they turned me down because I have high blood pressure. It must be a residual from the time I was in that damn concentration camp."

"What can we do?" The hoarseness in her voice could not disguise the tension she was experiencing.

"I am going on a diet of grapes and cooked white rice, three times a day. It is the only way I know how to cure hypertension. I've got everything to gain by trying it."

She did not feel it necessary to tell him she had passed the test, and he didn't ask.

After Kristallnacht, conditions grew considerably more threatening for anyone not fitting Hitler's Aryan model. The Lewys came to a decision about Stephan and decided to tell him their plan for him when they picked him up for their weekly Sunday outing,

"You must know how greatly concerned we are for your safety as well as for our own with all those crazies around," Johanna started the difficult subject about to be discussed.

"So," Arthur continued, "we have decided to take advantage of a good plan offered through the orphanage."

"What kind of a plan?" Stephan's eyes darted back and forth.

"Auerbach has been given the opportunity to send you older children to France for security reasons. This plan will allow you to leave Germany immediately."

Stephen looked at them incredulously. The hairs on his body seemed to stand at attention, making his skin prickle and feel as if it were crawling. "What do you mean, leave Germany?"

"Don't worry, Hanusch. It will be okay. Other countries like Denmark, Norway, and Holland—even Belgium and England—they are all willing to admit German children who are thirteen years old and older as refugees. Paris is a wonderful city, and the experience will be interesting as well as good for you.

"Yes, my son, and we will feel at ease knowing you are safe."

"But what about you?" he asked through quivering lips.

"We will join you as soon as we can, maybe in America."

"You are going to America?"

"We will see. Nothing is definite yet. We might go to a place called Boston, in the state of Massachusetts. We will write each other."

So, on July 7, 1939, thinking of their son's protection, the Lewys, like many other families, took their fourteen-year-old son to the railroad station. They were sending him to the refuge of Paris on a children's convoy, called a Kinder transport, along with twenty other children from the orphanage. Before Stephan could leave, he and the other children had to obtain a government clearance affirming they owed no taxes.

At the train station, the adults joked and laughed and kissed their children goodbye, making it seem more or less as if they were sending their children off on a picnic. To avoid upsetting their offspring, and to hide any signs of sadness or fear, most of the parents smiled, joked, and promised their children, "We will see you soon." "…in a little while." "Be good children."

Realistically, the parents knew they might be saying their goodbyes with the possibility they will never be seeing their sons and daughters again.

Stephan was part of a group of about forty German children traveling without an escort to their new destination, somewhere in France. He now knew his parents were also planning to leave Germany, but he didn't know when or where.

The years Stephen spent in the orphanage conditioned him to live in large groups of children. He learned at a very young age how to cope, how to live in the present and how to conduct himself.

He heard his father's voice telling him, "Remember, you are a German. Act accordingly." Stephan did as he was told. He followed instructions, and he was determined to survive. In some areas, he was mature beyond his age.

As the train pulled out of the station, Stephan drew three x's in the dust, with his finger, on the last window of the train, a German superstition, signifying to him he would never return.

"I wonder if there will be anyone to meet us," Stephan said turning to his friend Henry as the train pulled into the Paris railroad station.

"There's someone over there with a sign. I think it's for us." Henry was right.

The man with the sign greeted the boys and helped them transfer to a local train headed for Quincy, a forty minute ride outside of Paris. They felt really excited when they arrived on the grounds of an authentic French castle, a former exclusive private school for girls. The boys all expressed their surprise.

"Wow," Henry whispered to Stephan. "Is this where we are going to live?"

"Quiet down, please," they were instructed, and like good German children, they obeyed. "The owner of this fine place is Le Counte de Monbrison," the person who had accompanied them said. "He is a man of great conscience, and we must not abuse his generosity. He and the niece of the Romanoff's, once the Czars of Russia, are trying to save lives."

The Count and the Russian woman were indeed altruistic. They felt their position required them to assist those less fortunate. At first they sponsored Russian children who were in danger. Then, when they heard some Spanish children were threatened by the Franco regime, they sent for them. Now they decided to sponsor a group of German boys trying to escape the Nazis. Their plan was to provide these boys with a roof over their heads as well as provide for their daily needs.

When they first arrived, however, the manor house was still occupied by female refugees from Franco's Spain, and there was no room for the forty newcomers.

"You will have to stay in a nearby place, Annex Garon, for a few days until the Spanish girls are placed elsewhere," the boys' supervisors were told.

After the girls were placed with French families, the new arrivals moved into the castle staffed by Russian refugees, personnel devoted to the Czar, another paradox Stephan met head on.

"The Czar and his loyalists had no love toward Jews. And it is obvious these instructors feel no affection for us," Stephan told one of the Auerbach boys.

The youngsters now had no religious connections as they did in Berlin, and they decided to hold their own religious services on the Sabbath and holy days without the support from those in charge.

All but one of the children in the group was Jewish. They asked among themselves, "How did this new boy get here in the home with us?" No one knew, but there he was.

"I think his father must have been a Communist, so he had to be constantly on the run from the Nazis," Stephan figured out, knowing his own father's experience.

Anyone who knew anything about the Nazis knew they were notorious for taking relatives hostage, especially the children of those who were attempting to elude arrest. The child-hostage would be released if and when the person being sought would surrender. They traded a parent for a child.

Unfortunately, the past finally caught up with the non-Jewish boy during the occupation when the Nazis intercepted him one day when he went into town. The father then turned himself in. The supervisors at the home received news a few months later both son and father were taken to a death camp. Neither survived.

The fighting war started on September 2nd 1939, just as Stephan's father had predicted.

Nearly a year later, in May of 1940, after waiting anxiously for months, Arthur received the report he was waiting for.

"Johanna, good news. I received notice from the consulate in today's mail. They are allowing me to undergo another physical examination. Let us hope…" He left the thought unsaid.

When he returned from the consulate, Arthur burst through the door of their apartment, planted a big kiss on Johanna's cheek, grabbed her around the waist, and sang in singsong fashion, "I've passed. I've passed. I actually passed." Breathless he panted, "Now, we must think of how and when we can leave.

"So soon? So fast?"

"Yes," he snapped. "I stopped on the way home and paid for passage on a ship scheduled to leave from Rotterdam, since we cannot go through Hamburg. There is no connection between the port of Hamburg and the United States."

"But what about Stephan?"

"It's impossible to communicate immediately. I'll try to reach him by mail, but we won't be able to wait to see if he receives the letter. We cannot even delay our departure if or until he answers. We must not hesitate too long or" Again a thought unfinished aloud.

The necessity of a hasty departure made it impossible to get directly in touch with their son in time to let him know they were leaving. And they did not yet know their American address.

"He'll be all right. In France, at least, he will be safe, and we will find out where he is and write to him once we have a permanent residence."

They were not allowed to take much with them—only ten Reich Mark which amounted to about four dollars. Except for their wedding rings, they had to turn in all their jewelry for the gold content before getting their passports. They managed to smuggle a few pieces of jewelry sewn and hidden in their clothing.

A week later they had packed one suitcase each, bought tickets, and took the train to Rotterdam. They went directly to the wharf, located their ship, and boarded the boat which would carry them to safety. As they sailed around the tip of southern England on their way to the States, the captain announced the sad news over the ship's intercom. "I'm sorry to announce that Germany has invaded Holland, Belgium and France."

Now, any chance of communication between parents and son Stephan came to an end.

Meanwhile, in Quincy, the French town prepared for the worst. Stephan leaned out the window at the sound of a voice of shouting, "Hear this. Hear this." It was the town crier, riding through the streets on a gray and white horse while beating two medium sized drums, one on each side of the animal.

"Hear this," he cried again, banging the drums with a large padded stick, first on one side, then the other. "Oh yea…oh yea…Hear this. In case of air raids…one siren means airplanes are near," he shouted over the noise of the drums. "Two sirens will be a warning to go to a shelter. Three sirens mean business—take cover!" He repeated his message while riding throughout the village.

The Nazis were now easily rolling through all parts of Western Europe, including France. One night, shortly after all the boys were in bed, a siren howled its message of death. The boys all jumped out of their beds, grabbed their robes, and scrambled for the shelter in the basement of the castle. Everyone, that is, except Stephan. As a good, obedient German boy, Stephan obeyed the rules.

"It's only the first siren. Where are you all going?"

The boys, ignoring his question, ran to safety. Stephan remained in bed trembling with fright.

Soon the bombs started to fall, and one could hear the French anti-aircraft guns ack-ack-acking their shells skyward.

"Where the hell is Stephan?" the person in charge asked the group in the shelter. He made his way back to the dormitory, looked over the beds and found Stephen still in bed, quivering.

"What are you doing in bed," he shouted at the frightened boy. "Didn't you hear the sirens?"

"Yes, sir, but I was waiting for the third..."

The instructor didn't pause for him to finish his sentence. He screamed at him in no uncertain terms, "Get the hell out of here!"

By the time the Lewys arrived safely in the United States, they were deeply troubled over the war news. Picked up at the dock by Johanna's relatives, Arthur rode suffering silently in his misery. They arrived at their hosts' home and were shown into an upstairs bedroom where they would be staying until they found it convenient to move.

When he and Johanna were alone, he paced the floor, nearly tripping over a throw rug. Johanna sat in the rocker near the window waiting for him to speak.

Finally, he said, "My God, Johanna, what did I do? I believed he would be safe in France, but they have already capitulated. Paris has fallen. My poor son. What have I done?"

"It wasn't anyone's fault," she said trying to assuage his guilt.

"I am absolutely sick with worry. I feel so guilty. I thought we were surely doing the right thing."

"How were we to know?"

With the exception of Vichy France, in the southern part of the country, the Nazis now took over the entire land. The worried parents did not know where their son was, nor even if he were alive.

Feelings of fear filled their very being. Even so, Johanna tried to reassure Arthur that Stephan was safe, even if she did not believe it.

"Let's be practical for a moment," she said. "Now that we are here we must first find work so we can earn money. Then we can send for him."

"We'll have to find him first," was Arthur's cynical retort.

After working a short time in Haverhill, Massachusetts, an organization formed for the explicit purpose of helping refugees find employment. found the Lewys a new job in a Boston household on Beacon Hill. Their elderly employer, Mr. Block, had escaped from Czarist Russia and was now a successful executive in a profitable mining corporation. The only other members of the household were his adult nephew and Preston, the chauffeur. Working for Mr. Bloch gave Arthur a change of heart regarding his stereotype of Eastern Jews.

As Mr. Block told Johanna, "I had a dream that one day I would be driven to the Boston Red Sox and Boston Braves baseball games in a chauffeur driven car. And now, with my Negro driver, the dream has come true."

The Lewys were responsible for running the household in the Block's five-story brownstone home on Beacon Street.

Although Stephan and his parents lost complete contact with each other, his parents never stopped looking for him.

For Stephan, the transition from the orphanage in Berlin to the home in a suburb of Paris was not as traumatic as it was for some of the other children.

The years living without his parent's supervision had taught him it was best for his survival to transfer his father's authority to other parental figures. His father taught him to obey without question, as good German boys are all brought up and trained to do. It was as if he were gluing together his German demeanor to solidify his Germanic persona in order to blend in.

By now Stephan had developed a natural air of arrogance about him. He walked holding his head high, looking straight ahead. He had never associated himself with what his father referred to as foreign Jews, those who read the Yiddish language papers, or wore skullcaps, or draped themselves in prayer shawls and wore knotted strings hanging from under their vests. He was, after all, a German. His Judaism was secondary. He was taught to believe his attitude set him apart. A few times he even managed to fool the Hitler Youth who often failed to recognize him as their enemy.

Chapter Twelve

Even though I had completed the eighth grade in Germany, in France, because of the different language, I found myself back in the first grade studying French and elementary arithmetic. My French was poor at the time, but I was great in math and was able to advance rapidly.

By now we heard the Nazis were getting closer and closer to the French capital. As children, I don't think we realized that eminent danger was fast approaching. The Count, a French army officer, planned to join the Free French Army and strongly suggested our teachers should attempt to take us south, to Vichy, France, which was considered "Free France."

Our teachers took his advise. They managed to hire a wagon, and we all squeezed in.

"Be calm. Be calm," we were told.

"Why are they telling us to be calm?" we asked each other. Most of us were indifferent since we didn't know enough to realize how great a personal threat this was.

"The road sure is crowded," I said to Henry.

"I guess others have the same idea of getting to Vichy," I said.

"Wonder what's in Vichy," another boy added.

When we reached the Seine River one of our instructors saw an empty river barge and approached the ship's captain.

"I have forty children who need to escape the Germans and get to Vichy. Will you help us?"

"I have no love for the Germans. Get on board, quickly," he told us. "Get way in back on the bottom of the barge and keep quiet. I will cover you with a tarpaulin."

Now we knew why we were here. As we crouched down the thought finally occurred to most of us we were in great danger. When the tarpaulin threw us into a combination of darkness and lack of fresh air, we felt really terrified. Someone whispered, "Listen! Sounds like tanks."

Another added, "And motorcycles—passing by, I hope."

Some boys started to sob.

"Shhhhh."

My heart pounded so hard I thought if I don't quiet it down, we will all be caught. It was then, for the first time, I felt an overwhelming dread. We all were sweating and tense.

"What's going to happen to us?"

Again, "Shhhh. Nothing will happen if you keep quiet."

Then, we heard the staccato heels of boots hammering over our heads on the wooden deck.

"Oh, God," someone said.

I held my breath. We were all perspiring profusely. The barge cover was pulled aside with a cracking sound. The sunlight spread over what must have been our fearful upturned faces. As the warm air permeated the hole our hot bodies felt a chill. We looked up to see a group of German soldiers peering down at us. We stared at them. We held our breath, but we didn't utter a sound.

I heard one soldier say, "Whew. They stink like a bunch of Jew boys."

For some reason, unknown to any of us, they dropped the cover back over us and left. We all exhaled at the same time and said a silent prayer of thanks.

For us, our effort attempting to escape the Nazi invasion became a total disaster. There were so many barges trying to sail down the river, and the traffic were so jammed with anything that moved, roads leading toward southern France were paralyzed.

"Come on," our teacher told us. "Get off the barge. Quickly. We will have to start walking."

Where we were going none of us boys knew. The motorized German army had already passed by.

"It's useless to try to continue on," our instructors told us. "The wagon is gone, so we will have to walk all the way back to Quincy. Everyone stay together."

"But…" some boys protested.

"We have no choice."

To our surprise, when we arrived, exhausted, back at the chateau, we found a German calvary unit now occupying our former living quarters. A couple of the older boys, along with one of our directors, went to the group's commander and spoke to him.

When they finally came back, the director called us together. "I spoke with the Commandant…"

Someone interrupted him. "What did you say? What did he say?"

"Well, if you will be quiet, I'll tell you. I told him we are merely a group of young German refugee children, and this is where we have been living before…"

"Well, we live here now," he imitated the Commandant, and we laughed. "If you are willing to do some odd jobs for us, you can stay in the basement. One bit of trouble and out you go."

We felt temporarily relieved. Just like the other soldiers who discovered us in the barge, these men evidently wanted to win their war and just go home. They had no quarrel with us. Perhaps they did not realize we were Jewish.

So, while the German soldiers lived upstairs, we moved some extra beds down to the basement. Somehow we all got along. If they really knew we were Jews, then why were we not transported back to Germany as others were? Only God knows.

We were always hungry. "Can you smell that?" I asked Henry. "It smells like roasting meat."

"Oh, I'm so hungry. I could eat the fumes," he answered.

As one of my duties, along with some other boys, I was assigned to handle the soldiers' laundry. We put the clothes into a huge pot of water on the stove, added some soap the Germans had given us, and we boiled everything.

"Carry the pot over to the wash sink when it cools a bit and empty it over the sink. And be careful not to scald yourselves."

After we poured the hot water out, we added clean water to rinse the wash. Once, while we were doing the laundry, we noticed little specks of what looked like food floating in the water. "Look at that! The soldiers' cook must have forgotten to clean some food off the linens by mistake."

How gullible. Being without food much of the time, and feeling famished all of the time, we started eating these specks.

When our instructor caught us he asked, "What are you doing?"

"We found specks of food, and we are hungry."

"Idiots! Those specks are from the T-shirts. They disintegrated in the boiling water and shredded into pieces. It is not food."

By now we had grown into a very close knit group, and all of us seemed to be in a survival mode which somehow might have led to a fight I had with Henry, one of the boys and my only real friend. I don't remember what precipitated it. It might have been his remark I was not really Jewish because my mother was not, but I remember my voice when I reacted. It didn't seem to be coming from me. The sound from my throat sounded like an animal growling. I pulled out my pocket knife and grazed him across the knuckles.

"What the hell are you doing?" he yelled.

"I...I..." I stuttered. I was surprised at myself.

After the fight, he was bleeding and had to go for first aid. I do not recall ever feeling so violent before or since. I felt disgusted with myself. What would my father say if he knew?

.

It was early in the fall of 1940 when our supervisors gathered us together. "We are going to Paris," he said with a smile on his face.

"Who is going," I asked.

His answer, "All forty of us," was greeted with a loud cheer.

I was suspicious and did not hesitate to ask, "Why?"

"Be quiet," and "Who cares?" was the response from the boys.

So, for reasons we were not told, we were taken to Paris where we were housed for three wonderful weeks in a rented three-story Parisian building.

"Hey, this is really great," we all agreed, even though the German army occupied the city and were very visible. No one bothered us, which was another miracle in my life.

The thing I remember most about my Paris adventure was the food. Black olives were almost the only available food for the whole week, but these were nourishing enough, so we didn't starve. However, the past still influences me. To this day I will eat only green ones.

At the end of the three weeks, as we were about to be put on a truck to go on what we thought was an outing, my cousin Gunther called me aside which surprised me, since we rarely exchanged confidences.

He told me, "I'm not going with you when you leave."

"What do you mean you're staying?"

"I met this gorgeous lady, and she's invited me to stay with her. I'm not going to pass up an opportunity like this," he whispered to me. "I'm leaving now."

I tried to convince him he should not do this, but his stubborn streak was like a rip tide pulling him in over his head. He would not listen to me.

He hooked up with this much older woman, and to my way of thinking, she took him in for other than altruistic reasons. Maybe she even thought he was older, or maybe she was flattered by his youthful attention. He told me years later he stayed in German occupied Paris until Maria got them both a visa for the America.

In all probability, because of the German occupation, Gunther was able to communicate with his mother in Berlin. My Aunt Maria, whom I called Aunt Mimi, was a remarkable attractive woman. In her younger years she had bit parts in German films. Perhaps because she was so good-looking and maybe because she extended many "personal favors," she escaped being arrested, and finally received the visas they needed.

Leaving Gunther behind, we finally arrived at what was to be our first destination, still unaware of where we were or why.

"Okay, boys. Get off the truck and follow us," our leaders

instructed us. "Hurry."

"Oh, God, look," someone said.

"This is the border into Vichy France," I yelled.

We all got very excited when we saw we were about to walk across the border into "Free France," and we started to cheer as we ran.

Safely over the border, our instructor pointed to a dilapidated old vehicle which looked as if it were incapable of moving ten passengers, let alone forty enthusiastic boys. "Okay, everyone get on the truck," he shouted.

It took us three hours to arrive at our new destination, the city of Limmoges, in St. Pierre de Fursac, located in the Creuse district in central France.

"Here we are, boys," we were told. "We are at the Chateau de Chabannes, compliments of OSE, the French organization formed specifically to rescue you children."

Our instructor informed us, "Listen now. Everybody over the age of thirteen must go to the ORT school in the barn on the property of the castle."

"What is this…this…ORT school?" one of the older boys asked.

"It stands for the Organization for Rehabilitation through Training. Primarily it's a teaching facility for refugees. They will teach you a trade which will provide you a means to earn a living so you can become independent."

"Does everyone have to do this?" an eight-year-old whined.

"No. Part of the barn will be converted to a school for you younger children."

We were told their motto was, "A trade, unlike a profession, does not require knowing a foreign language. Anyone with a skill or trade has a better chance to survive in most situations."

I told a friend, "I don't think this is what my father had in mind for me as a career."

We both laughed.

All the necessary machines and cutting tables were available to us. And so we learned a trade.

"I'm not sure how making a pen holder is going to help me survive," I told my friend, "but at least it keeps me from going crazy with boredom."

I didn't enjoy making comb holders, or pocketbooks or wallets, but I think I was quite good at it simply because my father taught me to do my best consistently, and I was determined to do just that. I even felt a kind of satisfaction, in a way, because when I was told to do something, I did it, and did it well.

Living conditions in the Chateau were miserable, but at least we had a roof over our heads. Food was very scarce. We often joked about whose stomach growled the loudest. For breakfast we did have a small amount of milk and bread which tasted like it was made with a mixture of mostly sawdust and barely any flour. It was supplied by a local baker. Once a week, on Sunday, we had about two small size cubes of meat. I swallowed my portion so fast I didn't even taste it.

"I think we better find a way to get some food, even if it means going out at night to steal what we can find," I suggested.

"Hey," Fritz told me, "I found a farm nearby. Let's sneak over tonight and see what we can find."

"First, let's see if we can find some sacks to put the food in," I suggested. My father had drummed into me to always be prepared.

We all thought that was a good idea. When it got dark, we crept into the fields.

"Cram whatever food you find into the bags. Hurry," I whispered.

We scrambled all over the field, bumping into each other in the dark, laughing as though we were on a picnic.

"You better keep the noise down," I whispered. "Fill the sacks with whatever you find. We'll sort the stuff out later."

We managed to find some apples, turnips, pears and corn, a good haul. The first thing we did when we returned to the castle was to slice the turnips as fast as we could and slap the pieces onto the sides of the hot stove where they stuck until they were roasted. We gobbled the pieces up as soon as we could get the hot pieces in our mouths.

Sometimes we took a rickety old two wheel cart, pulled by an ox, to the surrounding farms, and tried to purchase some potatoes. Of course, buying this so called contraband was illegal.

"I don't care if it is illegal. All I know is I'm hungry," Fritz grumbled.

We took up a collection amongst ourselves and managed to gather a few coins from the money we had earned doing odd jobs. We knew of a friendly farmer and offered him the small amount we had collected. "Come. I will help you fill the cart with potatoes. Hurry up before someone sees who shouldn't."

"Ichhh. Look at my hands. They're covered with dirt," one of the more fastidious boys cried.

"Never mind that. Help cover the potatoes with hay.

"If you are hoping nobody will discover what you actually have hidden underneath all that hay, it won't work," the farmer who sold us the contraband whispered, shaking his head. "Anyone can tell from the type of noise those squeaking wheels make that you have a heavy load under all that hay."

"I don't care," I told the man. I remember my father telling me "you'll never get anywhere unless you are willing to risk."

"We'll take our chances anyway," I told the farmer.

Fortunately, we did not get caught, and we survived on huge amounts of turnips and potatoes. "It's not the most appetizing of meals," someone observed.

"Yeah, but at least we eat three times a day," I answered.

The smell of the vegetables, especially the turnips was sickening, but the prized booty kept us from starving. Need I say, today turnips are not one of my favorite vegetables, and I avoid them at all costs?

Our physical living conditions were primitive. We older boys slept in an unheated dormitory over the barn which was full of what seemed to us to be foot long rats. It wasn't too unusual to have their company in our beds every now and then.

We started to play a game. When we got into bed, we covered ourselves completely with our blankets, and if we felt one of those creatures running over us, we waited until it got near our arm. Then, while still covered, we raised our arm vigorously, and the rat went flying over to someone else's bed. The shrill screams were heard throughout the building. It was a diversion.

Besides using the pot bellied stove in the center of the room for "cooking" slices of turnip, we also used it for heat when we were lucky to find something to burn.

"If we are going to keep warm, we have to get some wood to burn," I told the boys.

"Yeah? And where do you think we are going to get it?" Hans, the practical one asked in a sarcastic tone he didn't even try to disguise.

"We'll just have to go to the nearby forest," I answered, ignoring his contemptuous tone of voice.

"Oh yeah? And what if we're caught?" Erich asked.

"We'll deal with that if and when we have to. Meantime, we have to do something," I answered, "or we'll all freeze. Besides, it will be less risky if we sneak over when it gets good and dark."

"Okay, lets go," Fritz prompted eagerly.

About ten o'clock that night, five of us boys sneaked to the edge of the wooded area and immediately started to chop down some trees with two old axes we found in the barn. I don't know if it was unadulterated fear or the fact it was just below freezing that we were shaking. We were as quiet as we could be, but how inconspicuous could we be hacking down trees?

The farmers who must have used these woods as their own source of fuel heard us, and they started shooting their guns in the air, trying to scare us off. They knew who we were, and we felt grateful they didn't try to kill us.

I learned to function in a routine the few years I lived with my parents and at the orphanage, so it wasn't difficult for me to adapt. Now, we started in the morning, after we got out of bed, to first eat our meager breakfast, and then, since there was no running water inside, we were instructed by the matron, "Go outside to the pump and wash yourselves thoroughly, and be quick about it before you do your chores. Remember, cleanliness is next to Godliness."

Needless to say, there is no way we would not be quick, since we had to stand by the pump, half naked in the very cold autumn and winter mornings, to wash ourselves with soap made mostly of non sudsing sandstone. Even though the matron insisted cleanliness was part of being spiritual, we certainly didn't feel the necessity, nor were we motivated to keep clean.

The matron made sure we kept busy during the day. "Each of you will have an assigned duty which will be periodically rotated," she instructed us. Among our chores were washing and sweeping floors, and serving at tables. We also started to plant vegetables in a big area behind the Chateau in the late fall for spring and summer harvesting.

"Gosh, this stuff stinks," I complained, not at all thrilled when it was my turn to mix the cow and horse dung in the soil for fertilizer. It sure was a different experience for us city boys, but when everything was growing, I realized it was much easier and safer than stealing.

After completing my chores I went to my leather working lesson. The younger children attended school taught by some of the older residents.

Our only entertainment was going out for walks. It was then we had opportunities to mingle with children of the town. We played football (soccer), volleyball and other games with them, and in the summer we used to swim in a little pond further down the road.

"Gee," some of us commented when we first went swimming, "the ground under the water sure feels nice and spongy on our feet."

"It should," one of the town's children told us. We found out in short order the pond with the nice, spongy bottom was shared with the local cows. Besides drinking from the pond, they did whatever else they needed to do. It made for an uncommonly soft lake bottom on which to walk.

"What the hell. I'm not going to let this stop me from swimming," one of the boys said as he laughingly waded into the water. We all followed.

About this time, some of us discovered girls. There was a great deal of competition among the fifteen senior boys for the attention of two older girls who lived in another dorm.

One girl, called Angel, was my first love. I'm sure I wasn't the only boy in her life, but she and I used to go off walking in the woods, innocently kissing under the trees. To us, it seemed very romantic. Years later we had the opportunity to take the same walk again as adults, when a group of us had a reunion in St. Pierre de Fursac.

Linens were changed only once a month. "Fold the dirty sheets, boys," we were told, "and push them down into these big sacks, then heave them into the wagon." Since we had no soap, someone was hired to deliver the linens to the closest commercial laundry, fifty miles away.

The huge sinks where laundry was washed were located on the first floor of the barn. There was also storage space and a doctor's office somewhere in another corner. Proper sanitary conditions were lacking, and because of it, we were all subjected to various types of ailments. It was a continuous problem. Fortunately, one of the counselors with us had some medical training, which we sometimes had to utilize. He recognized when I needed medical attention, and he called in the local doctor.

"I'm afraid you've picked up a bad staph infection, boy," the doctor told me when I developed several boils over my body about the size of half a lemon.

"Sorry, Stephan," the doctor told me, "but now that the boils are large enough, I'm afraid we are going to have to apply hot compresses until the boils turn black on top."

"But why." I was scared.

"Then we can peel off the tops and let the puss escape."

I screamed a few times. It hurt like hell. I was given some kind of medication which was supposed to prevent these infections, but it seemed to work only occasionally.

We learned to invent ways to get along in our daily lives. I developed a rather unique approach of supplying myself with food.

Paper goods were in short supply, so there was a daily paper distribution. We were allocated three square pieces of toilet paper daily, and since I was constipated most of the time, I didn't need them every day.

"Listen," I would say, approaching one of the boys, "I'll trade you my three pieces of toilet paper for your bread."

Since our dorm had no toilet facilities, we had to walk into the next building, which at times, wasn't always a comfortable stroll when it was winter. So, another example of improvising, for convenience, we "used" the open window. We got out of bed, went to the window and did what had to be done.

When we first settled in, one fellow had the unfortunate habit of innocently parking his brand new bicycle outside, under this window. One morning when he went outside and saw his bicycle he got extremely angry, and we heard him yell, "Who the hell shit on my bicycle?"

Chapter Thirteen

It had been over two years since Stephan had seen his parents. He finally decided to face the possibility that his parents might be dead when he approached the person in charge of his group.

"I see it has been quite a while since you have been in touch with your family. What kept you from trying to locate your parents before this?" the director asked Stephan.

"I don't know. Maybe I was afraid—afraid maybe they might be dead or afraid I failed my father in some way. I don't know. Anyway, I am willing to find out the truth now. Can you help me find my parents?"

Stephan and the other boys had no idea how barbaric the Nazis were behaving toward the Jewish people in Germany, and in the lands they invaded.

"I know my parents wanted to go to America, and if they could, they planned to go to my mother's distant cousin in Massachusetts, in a place called Haverhill." Stephan's mouth went dry. He could feel the hair tingling on the back of his neck. He blinked hard to avoid crying when he had no answers to all the questions he was asked.

"If they are still in Germany, they probably will be in Berlin. Otherwise, they might be somewhere near Boston, in America. I just don't have any address."

"You don't sound very certain. Well, I'll see what I can do. It will take time."

The director contacted the Red Cross in Switzerland. They located a copy of the Lewy's affidavit and found the name Klapper on it, which must have been Johanna's cousin's name. Mentioned on the document was an address in Haverhill, Massachusetts. The Red Cross then got the full address, and Stephan was notified.

"You mean…they may be here…at this address?" The weight of anticipation which lay so heavily on his shoulders lifted. He felt if he didn't hold onto something, he would float, he was so happy. "How can I reach them? What do I do? Can I go there?" he shot questions at this teacher without taking a breath.

"Whoa…whoa. Take a breath, young man. First, you must sit down and write them a letter. Then we will try to send it to them through the auspices of the Swiss Red Cross."

"I'll do it. I'll do it…right now!"

"Johanna, there's a letter here from Switzerland. It's been forwarded from Haverhill to our address here in Boston."

"Yes, I saw it. It is addressed to you."

"What do you think it means? I'm afraid to open it. You open it." His hands were shaking.

"No. It is addressed to you." Johanna tried to hide her own apprehension as she peeled potatoes for dinner.

With trepidation, Arthur opened the envelope.

"Oh, my God," Arthur cried out. "It's…it's from Stephan. Johanna, he's alive."

They grabbed each other and danced and laughed and cried with relief. "Now we…oh God…we must find a way to get him here now…at once." Arthur sputtered.

"First thing we must do is write to him and tell him we are in Boston and have received his letter and how thrilled we are…." Johanna gasped, wiping her eyes.

Weeks after his father mailed the letter, Stephan was called into the director's office. "I think this is for you."

"It's a letter from America! My God, it's from America!"

"Well, aren't you going to open it?" his instructor questioned.

"I don't know…I'm so…excited. Sure, I'm going to open it," and he continued to stare at the envelope. Stephan rarely showed his emotions, but this was overwhelming.

"If you aren't going to open it, I will."

"No…no, I'll open it." Then he started to read to himself.

Dearest Stephan,
We were so excited when your letter came we first sat and stared at the envelope before we dared to open it.

He looked up from the letter and told his instructor, "They write of their excitement and their love and how they are going to find a way to have me come to America."

And for the first time in years, Stephan allowed himself to cry.

Chapter Fourteen

The day started off badly. In the morning delivery of the mail, a letter arrived from Washington, D.C. addressed to Arthur Lewy. It read, "This is to inform you that the visa for Stephan Lewy has been denied."

"What did they say?" Johanna asked in disbelief.

"That's ridiculous! What can possibly be their reason?" the shocked parents asked each other shaking their heads.

"What did they say was the justification for this?"

"They didn't give one."

"This is outrageous," Johanna practically screamed.

"We must get some advise," Arthur decided, "At once!"

When they called a friend and asked him how they should go about things, he proposed, "The best thing you can do is to get in touch with the International Institute."

"What is that?"

"It's a group which serves as a huge support system for those of us who still have relatives in Europe, and it so happens, it's located right down the street, six blocks away from where you live. I think you might do well to get involved with them."

As soon as Arthur hung up, he told Johanna, "Come, Let's go...now."

They quickly put on their coats and hats. Johanna grabbed her pocketbook, and they rushed out the door.

The first thing the person at the Institute advised was, "Hire an attorney who deals with such cases." They were given several names of lawyers to call.

The first advise they received from the lawyer they hired was "We must go to Washington where we will plead your only son's case in person."

In Washington, they met with defeat.

"How can they turn our appeal down? On what grounds?" Arthur asked the lawyer. They felt as if they were climbing the slippery slope on a mountain of bureaucracy.

The lawyer just shook his head, bewildered. "Is there anything in your past that would make them turn him down?"

Arthur thought for a moment that maybe it was because he had been a Socialist, but rejected the possibility.

"No...no," Arthur and Johanna echoed in a chorus.

Johanna started to weep in quiet desperation, "I don't know what we can do next, but we must do something."

They returned to Boston, and when they told their friends the bad news, an acquaintance suggested, "Go to one of the coffee klatches held by members of the Immigrant Mutual Aid Society (IMAS). They can do the impossible."

"Yeah, he is right. The members exchange information and leave no possibilities undone, especially when it came to locating and possibly saving a child," their friend, Mrs. Golden, insisted.

At one of the meetings, it was proposed that Johanna write as poignant a letter as she could to President Roosevelt himself.

And she did.

Dear Mr. President,

Our only child already has an affidavit signed by a friend of ours, and he desperately needs to be granted a visa by the United States government allowing him to join us, his parents, and save him from living in Nazi occupied Europe where he certainly is at risk of losing his young life. We applied for the visa and were refused. No explanation was given to us for not granting permission for the visa.

My dear President Roosevelt, our only child is good, honest and smart, and I promise, if our son is granted a visa to this wonderful country, he will make the very best soldier in the American army.

She signed it with her name and added, "from a future American Citizen."

They spent many anxious weeks waiting for a reply. They could hardly ignore the headlines blaring their daily isolationist messages. "Europe for the Europeans" and "It Is Not Our War."

It was America's nationwide attitude, nourished and stoked on the flames of fear and covert anti-Semitism.

They read in the local paper what some columnists were saying. "If refugees are allowed into our country," they wrote, "they will compete with American workers for jobs which are not yet plentiful." Another wrote, "Those people have ways that are foreign to us."

Arthur knew Roosevelt read the papers and was fully aware that many Americans felt this way. "We know," he told Johanna, "the president is a political animal and wants to be reelected, which means he is not included to help the European Jews to come to America."

The President never answered, at least not directly, but seven weeks later, Stephan was notified he had a visa waiting for him in the city of Lyon, France. Johanna always suspected Mrs. Roosevelt saw her letter and was influential in getting the necessary visa.

I was now seventeen. Although I wanted to be reunited with my parents, I felt almost disloyal leaving my friends behind in Chabannes. By early 1942, my parents were sending me little postal notes which sometimes were worth one dollar and sometimes five dollars. They figured I could use the money.

Even as an adult, thoughts still invade my memory—thoughts of my past experiences that faintly whisper in my mind about how far from unworldly I must have been.

I had been able to escape danger several times, and managed to survive. But, like many others, I did not understand then just how serious the situation was in Germany as well as in the rest of Europe. I just did not—could not—fathom how perilous the circumstances were. So, when it came time to pick up my visa I wrote to my parents and asked, "Could I possibly wait another six months. I want to buy myself a bicycle."

Unreal? Crazy? For sure, but I think I was just acting on the part of me that was still an uninformed, unsophisticated boy in my teens. Gullible? Certainly. Ironic? Absolutely. I was still childlike, although mature enough in the art of survival.

The next letter I received from my father was an appropriate and uncompromising reply. It read, "Damn it, you be on that next transport or forget your visa."

I soon started to receive letters regularly from my parents. Mutti wrote me that one of her sisters finally was able to escape from Germany and sail to Argentina with their mother.

I read, "She accepted a marriage of convenience by mail from a total stranger, a German refugee living in Buenos Aires. When the ship arrived in Argentina, he boarded the ship, and they were married by the captain."

Gee, I thought as I read, *things must have gotten pretty bad in Berlin since I left. What a strange way to get married.*

Now I was on a road to a new adventure. To receive my visa I had to travel alone from the Chateau de Chabannes south to Lyon. When I arrived at the U.S. Consul's office to pick up my papers, the clerk looked puzzled.

"It seems you have no citizen status, not even here in France."

"Yes, sir. I know. Germany took away my citizenship. I have been living here in France these past few years."

"I will see what I can do for you. It will take time. Please wait."

After waiting an hour, an hour of uncertainty, an hour not knowing what my future might hold, a sudden wave of nausea engulfed me. I couldn't catch my breath. Why are they keeping me waiting so long? What if they cannot—or worse—will not—help me? I inhaled deeply with relief when help finally arrived after I waited several hours.

"You are a very lucky boy. After I explained the situation to my superior, he contacted the French government, and in its generosity, the powers that be have invented a unique stateless passport for you."

So saying, the clerk handed me a fancy decorated paper, bordered in red with the necessary passport information. I marveled at the enormous significance this small beautiful piece of paper had to my very survival.

Chapter Fifteen

To board a ship for America I had to get to Marseilles, where I was fortunate to find a place to stay with a relative of parents of one of the children housed at the home in Chabannes.

In Europe, countless people created "bedrooms" out of the space located under staircases, so I didn't think it unusual when she told me, "I'm sorry we don't have anything else." Madame Argent apologized for the little 6 X 3 cubby hole which was to serve as my bedroom.

"Please do not apologize. I am grateful I have such a nice place to stay," I told her. "And your relative said you are an excellent cook."

The desire to be reunited with my family gnawed at my fertile imagination. I began to realize how deeply meaningful the pending possibilities were for me. I shared some of my concerns with Madame Argent.

"My father married my second mother, Johanna, just about a year before they sent me to France."

"Are you afraid you won't like each other?"

"Oh no, Johanna is wonderful. I just feel nervous when I think about them…not about whether they are living comfortably, or if they own an automobile…but more about will they look different, you know, old. And how their health is, and will we recognize one another. You see, I haven't lived at home since I was six, and"

"Have either of them been in ill health?" Madame Argent interrupted my babbling.

"All I know is what I learned through their letters. My father has recovered from another heart attack."

"You have been all right so far. I am sure the good Lord will look after you all a bit longer."

"Sorry, there are no ships scheduled this week," I was told over and over again.

It turned out I had to wait nearly seven weeks until transportation turned up. But at least now I felt I was moving one step closer to being reunited with my parents.

Marseilles seemed to me to be a city much like Paris in more ways than one. Although this part of France was supposed to be unoccupied, the Vichy government here had an even more pro-German attitude than the Germans, if that is possible.

My host warned me, "You had better be careful. This so-called Vichy government has a bad record of collaborating with the Nazis."

I didn't know it at the time, but they were the only nation in all of Europe whose local authorities voluntarily deported Jews without the presence of German occupying forces. How I escaped this horror I cannot imagine, unless, as I suspect, my excellent command of both French and German, plus my Germanic demeanor might have been my saving grace. Today this legacy of collaboration still remains a source of tension in France.

This area of France had not yet been touched by the destruction of war, but it was hard hit economically. I could tell by the prices of necessities rising daily. Meat and dairy were expensive, if one could find any. Fortunately for me, at least, I usually found some sweets which satisfied my hunger and which I enjoyed.

Every morning, after a skimpy breakfast of ersatz coffee and a roll, I walked over to the harbor and check with a refugee organization with my usual question. "Is my ship scheduled to arrived today?"

Always I heard the same answer, "Sorry, not today."

And when it was not on the schedule, I spent the day walking around by myself, enjoying the warmth of the wonderful southern French sunshine, going back to where I was staying to have lunch, then exploring more of the city before returning for dinner. My landlady was very skilled in getting food. I don't know how she did it, but there was enough food to keep us from starving.

Now, as each day passed, my aristocratic attitude started to change, and my patience started to wear down. I noticed my normal, pleasant nature began to transform into one of anger and irritability. And what was most frustrating was I had no one and nowhere to direct my anger.

I suffered anxiety and confusion. I felt lethargic, powerless and flustered all at the same time. It was not a good position to be in, especially for one not yet seventeen. The only way I could comfort myself was when I could conjure up the thought of eventually seeing my parents again.

When I could be more rational and less self-absorbed, I became aware there was something terribly weird about this city, something I could not put my finger on at first. After a while I realized what it was.

"Madame Argent, I notice there are no young boys and young men around."

"There are several possibilities," she answered. "Some could be away in the army. They could have been killed by one side or another, or most likely they were simply turned over to the Nazis by this pro-German government."

The thought made me shudder. I don't know why no one ever questioned me as I walked around the city. My luck was holding up, I guess.

Now, since it had been decided for me by my father that I would not buy the bicycle I wanted with the money he had sent, I had some extra money in my pocket, and I could afford to buy extra food for Madame Argent and me when I could find any. When there was no word about a ship, I wandered around until I found these sweet smelling specialty bakeries. They always seemed to have enough sugar to make little individual round cakes with lots of raisins in them. I always bought one or two each day to satisfy my sweet tooth.

I had time to sit on a bench looking out to sea wondering, *Were my father and mother healthy? Did Johanna like where they were living? Would I get along with my father and would he treat me differently now that I am older? What were they doing?* These thoughts went around in my head like a carousel without the music.

Finally, after weeks of waiting, I saw my name listed on a French freighter's manifest sailing early the next morning. Suddenly, I felt a surge of energy. I practically flew back to my room. I threw some of the few things I had accumulated into a suitcase. I said goodbye to Madame Argent. I kissed her and thanked her, and then I rushed back down to the dock and boarded the ship, my ticket to freedom. My heart thumped so hard my ribs began to hurt. I thought, *If I don't calm down, my heart will burst.*

By now, the Lewys were in touch with HIAS, the Hebrew Immigrant Aid Society. Every day they inquired if Stephan's ship had arrived in Marseilles. Their son did not know that he would not be allowed to board the ship until HIAS received the $500 fare from his parents, at which time they would be advised of when the vessel was scheduled to leave port.

Chapter Sixteen

Much to my surprise, we sailed east from Marseilles, along the French coastline. I had no idea why we were heading in that direction instead of going west to America, but I couldn't find anyone who knew, and who would volunteer the information. I finally managed to speak with the ship's radio man.

"The so-called Free French part of France is now totally occupied and under the domination of the Nazis. I don't think I will be going home any time soon," he sighed.

It seemed as though my luck was holding up. I was still two steps ahead of them. "But why are we heading east?"

Then he told me, "We are on our way to Barcelona."

"What are we going to do in Spain?" I asked. I figured he knew more than most because of his job.

"Well," the Frenchman told me, "if you must know, we are going to pick up passengers."

That satisfied my curiosity for a time. When we reached Barcelona, I discovered the purpose of our trip. The captain told those on board, "We are rescuing forty children of Spanish Communists who fought against Spain's dictator, Generalissimo Franco. They are in danger of being either killed or imprisoned."

This announcement at least told me they too were escaping from a totalitarian government, and like I, they were seeking refuge in America.

Since they were all much younger than I, the people in control of the ship put me in charge of these kids. I spoke no Spanish, just French and German. They spoke no French or German, only Spanish. Somehow, we managed to communicate. One of my duties was to get them to breakfast.

"Breakfast everyone," I told them. No one moved. When I pantomimed, putting a spoon to my mouth, one of them shouted. "Ahh, desayuno."

So I learned a new word—desayuno, breakfast in Spanish.

I also had to see to it that they stayed in their cabins to rest occasionally, and not run around all day throughout the ship. They were made aware of the importance of our voyage and were completely respectful and cooperative. To them this was one big picnic.

As we sailed west, we hugged the coast of France. I was told if a French freighter, such as ours, were to go out into the open sea, the Germans would surely torpedo it.

To put us somewhat at ease, we were told, "At least traveling this way, if the ship gets torpedoed, we have a chance of reaching the shore." Although that philosophy was not comforting, none of us felt in too much danger, possibly because we were young and too ignorant of seriousness of the situation.

While crossing the Mediterranean, a trip free of incident, we finally landed in Rabat, Morocco, where we were to be transferred to a neutral ship which would carry us the rest of the way. From the port, we were taken by bus from Rabat to just outside the city of Casablanca to wait for our ship. I looked around the dormitory where we were to be billeted. All I saw were walls lined with bunk beds.

Three or four of us older German speaking boys decided to make our way into the city of Casablanca. The experience left us with a memory none of us will ever forget.

We rode in an ancient dusty bus with strange looking objects that looked like stoves attached outside on the back of the vehicle.

"Hey, where is everybody going?" I asked my companion, as people were suddenly scrambling out of the bus.

"I don't know, but let's do whatever they do."

Each of the suitcases from the luggage rack on top of the bus was being thrown inside where the seats were.

One French speaking native explained, "There is no petrol, so they burn some type of compound gas to generate the energy from the stoves to propel the bus. The bus gets unbearably hot, so we all sit on top, outside."

"You went where?" the people in charge yelled at us hysterically. When we explained to the person in charge, he told us in no uncertain terms, "Are you crazy! That city is an incubator for germs. You could have gotten a terrible disease or worse. You could have been murdered. My God, you should never have taken such a risk."

I guess we were lucky because we maintained our health as well as our lives.

It was a Friday afternoon when I decided to take a walk around the city, near where we were staying. To my surprise, I discovered the city had a section crowded with Jews, probably originally from Spain. I recognized their stores from the various signs, "Strictly Kosher," painted in several languages.

The humid weather felt oppressively hot and sticky, and my shirt, moist with perspiration, clung to my back. In spite of my physical discomfort, I managed to find the market fascinating.

Fish in water barrels and other types of foods displayed on street carts were lying unprotected from the hot sun. The strong food odors, mixed with the high humidity, violated my nostrils, making each breath extremely painful to the senses.

As the sun began to set and the Sabbath approached, the market became more crowded. People were taking advantage of the prices of food quickly falling lower and lower. Pious Jews sold nothing after sundown, the start of the Jewish Sabbath, so they had to get rid of their merchandise.

I was so busy taking in all the sights that I didn't dwell on the fact I would soon be seeing my parents. I walked by what for me seemed to be an unusual looking building. Four stone pillars stood majestically outside a building presumably holding up the ancient structure's roof. Suddenly, I realized this was no ordinary building. It was a synagogue, one like I had never seen before. Its picturesque and charming style of Spanish combined with African architecture was very impressive.

When I ventured inside, I saw the most religious Jews I had ever seen. These Sephardic Jews all wore black fezzes, the brimless, cone-shaped hats worn by Eastern Mediterranean men. As each man entered the synagogue to pray, I saw him kiss his hand and then touch a mezuzah, a capsule fastened to the door post containing a small scroll inscribed with a handwritten part of Deuteronomy. The custom is prescribed in the Bible and is supposed to protect one's home from the plague.

As I looked down into the lower level of the building, I noticed a big slab of gleaming white marble. Seated cross-legged around it were several men praying in Hebrew. Each wore a tallith, the fringed, white religious shawl, which they use to cover their fez capped heads as their sign of respect to God. Not only is it a sight to behold, it also conveys a sense of being at home. It is heartwarming that no matter what synagogue a Jew enters, no matter in what country, the Hebrew prayers are the same.

Delayed in Morocco, we all had to wait about another five or six weeks before a Portuguese passenger ship, the Serpa Pinto, came in from Lisbon. This was the same ship which was later alluded to in the television version of "Winds of War." The script called for someone to say, "Look at this ship with all the people on it," referring to the Serpa Pinto. And the response was, "Yeah, they're all a bunch of refugees!"

When we boarded the ship in Casablanca, it was only half-filled to its capacity of about seven hundred grateful but destitute Jewish refugees.

I managed to speak to a few of these people as they stood by the ship's railing. "Oh yes," one man in a group told me, "those damned murdering Nazis still allowed those of us with visas to leave Germany, but only after paying the Nazi government all we own as the price for freedom."

"Well, even though finding refuge has left us financially destitute, at least we are alive, so we have nothing to complain about," a tall thin woman dressed in black addressed the group. In response, all the others murmured in agreement.

In order to survive, these evacuees chose to give up their once prosperous way of life so they could pay for the trip to Lisbon and freedom. I found out later the next voyage of the Serpa Pinto, unfortunately, carried only about one hundred passengers. The Nazis had changed the rules, and even money could not buy freedom.

After we sailed from Casablanca, we stopped at Flores. I think it is the western most Portuguese island in the Azores. From there, we started across the Atlantic.

By the spring of 1942, while I was sailing to the United States, America had already entered the war.

"We really appreciate your generosity in putting us up while we are waiting for Stephan," Johanna told their friends with whom they were staying in the Bronx. "We are so anxious to see him after so many years."

"There is nothing you can do but wait," their host told their apprehensive guests. "By the way, Hanna," calling Johanna by her pet name, "how is it your English is so much better than Arthur's?"

Arthur felt a bit indignant at this remark, and in a tone dripping of sarcasm, he answered, "Perhaps it is because she is ten years younger than I, and…"

Johanna interrupted, "And he was so busy with more important things he didn't have a chance to practice, and I did."

Their host did not take offense at Arthur's caustic remark.

"Johanna is very active with groups of English speaking people," Arthur added, sounding more contrite.

It was up to Johanna to scan the newspapers for ship arrivals and to make the necessary inquiries concerning docking schedules.

"We should go to the Brooklyn waterfront everyday and remain downtown for a few hours just in case we get word of Stephan's ship. At least it will give us something to do to pass the hour,s and we will be out of our host's way."

"I'm afraid, Hanna, our permission to stay here will run out before he gets here." Arthur was referring to the government permit required for enemy aliens, including German Jews, granting only a calculated and limited time away from where they lived.

"We'll face that if it happens, Arthur. Don't worry."

As we were speeding across the Atlantic, I was a bit unnerved by all the ship's lights blazing in the night. It was then I started to bite my nails. A few days out to sea I managed to meet one of the ship's friendlier officers who spoke French, and I questioned him, "Why do we have so many lights on?" In my naiveté I asked, "Are we afraid of hitting something?"

"We are neutral you see," he started to tell me, "and that is why we fly an extra large Portuguese flag so prominently with the lights glowing, so any vessel can see we are a neutral ship.

Just then, without warning, the constant thunder of the engines stopped. The silence was eerie.

"What's happening?" we asked each other. The hair on my neck and arms now stood at attention.

A German U-Boat had bobbed up on the ocean's surface and had signaled us to stop. They were going to board us. My breath now started to come in small gasps. It felt like I was being smothered at the hands of my enemies. When we saw the crew set out toward us in a small craft, I noticed I was dizzy and my head ached as if the air I was trying to breathe lacked oxygen. The intense feeling made me want to vomit. I asked myself, *Can I escape from them again?* My mouth went dry.

The German sailors soon approached our ship, boarded it, walked silently through it from top to bottom, returned to their ship and submerged. It seemed we were all holding our breath because when the Germans left, I heard a loud sound of air whoosh from several people standing nearby as they exhaled in relief. Why they allowed over seven hundred Jews to sail on remains a mystery.

I hoped I wasn't running out of opportunities.

The multilingual Captain, in order to put us at ease, explained in German, "Hab keine angst."

"Not to worry? Not to worry? Of course I worry," I replied. In Spanish, which many Portuguese people also speak, the captain also reassured the children from Barcelona "No se preocupe a niños."

Then he went on to explain in German to the majority of German passengers, "The reason they checked us out was they knew that when the United States was neutral, some American ships were suspected of secretly transporting ammunition to England in what they called peacetime ships. So, even though we are flying the neutral Portuguese flag, they may have suspected us of carrying contraband and wanted to check it out."

"I'm sure that is all it was," one of the older passengers agreed, putting us all at ease.

One of the Spanish boys said, "Espero exacto."

That Spanish I understood. "I hope he is right too," I said.

As we approached Bermuda, we were about to face yet another dilemma.

"Ahoy, there, Serpa Pinto," we heard. "You cannot go on. Our ships will escort you into Hamilton Harbor where your passengers will have to go ashore," the British Navy insisted.

When we docked, we were told, "The children will be taken to the island used by the Boy Scouts. The adults will be housed in hotels."

We all wondered why this was happening. Wasn't Bermuda on the Allies' side?

Our captain explained, "They must inspect every piece of luggage, test every bit of ladies' face powder and perfume. They want to be sure there are no explosives being smuggled in."

"On a bunch of Jews?" someone snickered. "This is ludicrous."

"But we are all trying to escape to safety," another of the passengers said, shaking his head in disbelief. "What's the matter with them?"

What the matter with them was it was wartime, and they were British.

Chapter Seventeen

Shyness was still Stephan's constant companion which kept him from making many friends among the younger passengers on the trip to the States. The seven days it took for the British to release the ship seemed endless for those onboard and for those who waited for the ship's passengers at the end of the journey. Stephan's anxious parents who were staying with friends in the Bronx could do nothing but wait.

In June of 1942, after the Lewys waited for several weeks in New York, the Serpa Pinto finally sailed into New York Harbor and slowed down in front of the Statue of Liberty for the passengers to get a good view. Now Stephan could feel the tension he had been carrying all these years melt away like snow in springtime. He noticed a certain warmth enveloping him like he had not felt since he had been hugged by his beloved mother as a child. At last he was able to release this German persona which accompanied him most of his life and which he felt kept him safe.

"This is it," Stephan said half aloud.

He didn't know whether to laugh or cry. He sighed. His eyes finally filled with tears, as did other people's eyes while standing at the ship's rail. The passengers on board stood silently, speechless.

The silence was broken when a little voice was heard. "Mire a la se–ora," one of the younger Spanish children said, pointing to the famous Statue of Liberty.

"Ella es una Americanas?"

"Of course she is an American," the little girl with long blonde hair told the girl next to her.

"Ohhh, ella parece mi madre," still another child cried, and so saying, burst into tears.

"No, she does not look like your mother. She is America's mother," one of the other children said, comforting the crying child.

There was excitement all over the decks as the ship started to pull into New York Harbor. The docks were swarming with people waving and shouting out names, hoping to be heard. Passengers onboard the ship were waving and yelling their own names to the enthusiastic crowds.

Then, soon after a government inspector left the ship, the passengers heard an announcement coming over the loud speaker from the coast guard cutter. The voice also reached those waiting ashore, and in unison, a loud groan blanketed the pier.

"At this time no one will be allowed to disembark. Some of our Spanish passengers have fevers. The American government is cautious on this point and has put the whole ship in quarantine."

The ones who understood English repeated what was said in both German and Spanish.

"What is the voice saying?" those who understood no English asked.

"À cul es incorrecto?.

"There is nothing wrong, is there?" one of the other Spanish children asked no one in particular.

"Vas ist los?" those experienced with disappointment asked.

"We've come so far, certainly nothing is wrong."

Happy sounds turned at first into stunned silence, then into groans of disappointment. The people on the dock felt terrified.

"What more can happen to them...to us?" they asked one another.

Several people started to cry. Men yelled their indignation to anyone within earshot.

An elderly woman, stood near the railing next to Stephan. In anticipation of coming to America, she was dressed in what finery the Nazis allowed her to take. "What are they afraid of," she asked, "that maybe we are carrying some esoteric European disease?"

His face glum, the corners of his mouth turned down, Stephan felt discouraged and angry…boiling mad angry. "Damn it," he swore to the young man on his right. "Here I am, within reach of seeing the parents I have not seen in over three years, and yet another barrier is placed in front of me."

The tension—chains he had unshackled only a few minutes before—encircled him once more. "Damn, damn, damn." With each "damn," he hit his right fist into the palm of his left hand. "When am I going to feel safe and part of a family again. Why is this happening?"

The elderly lady responded, "Who knows, my child? Who knows, but at least we are alive, and we are here."

The ship sat at the dock for two days, within sight of New York City and the majestic Empire State Building, until both children's temperatures returned to normal. Now they all were free to leave the ship.

The Spanish children walked timidly down the gangplank and were greeted enthusiastically with open arms by the smiling welcoming families who were taking them in. When Stephan recognized his father and mother, the defiance and hard exterior which had glued him together all these years cracked. Emotionally, he reverted back to when they had parted, and his wobbly legs barely supported him as he made his way down the gangplank. A surge of energy came from nowhere, and he started to run toward them. Ignoring his father's outstretched hand he threw his arms around both his parents, and in the process, nearly knocked them both over.

The three of them laughed and cried with joy and relief. At last, they were united—a family once more.

"Stephan." Arthur's voice was tinged with his old German authoritarian touch. "Straighten your tie and pull down your jacket."

"My God, you are all grown up," his mother said, patting him on the shoulder, ignoring Arthur's admonition. In her exhilaration, Johanna started to tell him of their plans using English and was met with a blank stare.

"Oh! Of course. Du hast kein wort verstanden dass ich gesagt, habe?"

"Of course he doesn't understand," Arthur said.

She started to speak all over again this time in German.

He answered in French saying, "It's okay, Mutti. I learned a little English in school. And now that I am here, I want to learn fast."

His startled parents cocked their heads as if trying to understand a language which was foreign to them. Then, when they realized they didn't understand French, they all burst out laughing.

They hugged again, and then his practical parents, after eyeing their son up and down, said, "What would you like to do first?"

"Well, I've grown a little since I first got these clothes," Stephan joked.

"Come, we are taking you to the nearest clothing store and buying you a real honest-to-goodness American suit."

Stephan thought it was good to hear, "we are taking you to the store." He was once again under his parents' care, and it felt warm and wonderful.

While riding the subway to the area where the Lewy's New York hosts had suggested they might shop. Arthur told his son, "You cannot imagine the worry you caused us and what we went through, first to find you, then to get you here once we located you. You have your mother to thank for this. She did all the work."

Stephan touched Johanna's arm. "Thank you, Mutti. You can't imagine how very lucky I feel," he told Johanna slowly, in English with a heavy German accent. Then he leaned over and kissed her cheek. Now he had so much to tell them. He reverted back to German. It was easier for him.

"Believe it or not, we never knew what was happening here or in Germany," he explained.

"What do you mean you did not know?" Arthur asked impatiently.

"At no time did they tell us any of they events occurring outside our area, I guess so we wouldn't be scared. I could not have imagined the danger and the seriousness of my own situation, but I'll tell you this," and he gasped for breath before he spoke with such emotion he nearly let his old guard down. "I never let people see how hungry I was, or how scared I was, or how tired. I only allowed them to see, how do you say, die Fassade—the facade, the wall—I hid behind, guarding my fears, controlling my emotions, and concealing my needs like you taught me, Papa, as a good German does.

"And would you believe, behaving like a proud German affected how people dealt with me, and to some extent, my conduct contributed to my survival. And I owe that to you, Papa. 'We must always conduct ourselves as proud Germans,' you drummed into me on our Sunday visits from Auerbach, remember?"

"Certainly, I remember. And it is good you remembered."

Stephan's voice lowered as he continued quoting his father. "'Our religion is separate from our nationality,' you said. 'Remember that always, and make sure you yourself make the distinction.'"

"That's correct."

They continued reminiscing.

"And do you remember what you told me when I asked you, 'what do you mean make the distinction?'"

"Absolutely," his father replied sternly. "I told you as German Jews we do not care to speak Yiddish or read a Jewish newspaper, at least in public for others to see and judge us. Those people who do such things or dress in their particular religious garments, we Germans consider them beneath us."

"Yes, and you told me how they make themselves separate. They do not live in the mainstream of our society. I remember you said they are not a part of us German Jews."

"I still believe most of 'those people,' don't have the education of a 'true' German, and particularly, they don't have the gentility. They are too busy praying," said his father, reaffirming his atheism.

Right or wrong, wearing this Prussian notion like a suit of armor gave Stephan the confidence he needed to survive.

After finishing their shopping, they carried their new purchases, Stephan's few belongings, and their own luggage, to Grand Central Station, where they boarded the train to Boston, to Stephan's new home.

Chapter Eighteen

"An enemy alien? You're not serious," I asked my father.

"I certainly am serious. The government will issue you a document similar to a passport."

"Yes," Johanna added, "and believe it or not, it will be pink."

"You are considered an enemy alien, and have to report to the FBI and register within twenty-four hours of your arrival in Boston," Stephan's father told him.

Germany made him stateless and now, as a German Jewish refugee; America made him an enemy alien.

As in Europe, where people carried identification on them at all times, now so too did Stephan have to carry this pink paper on his person constantly.

"Something else you should know," his father told him with a serious look on his face. "Before you arrived, our home was searched by the FBI at least three times."

"Why?" Stephan asked incredulously.

"I guess they were probably looking for Nazi connections."

"That's a joke, isn't it? A Nazi Jew?"

"No joke, Stephan," his mother assured him. "I was shaking like a bowl of gelatin.

"What did you do? Didn't it remind you of the SS coming?"

"Not quite. We were a bit tense," his father continued. "You should have seen their faces when they found three books with swastika symbols on them. They looked at me as if they had found a bomb.

"Those books are about the German Olympics. I said to them, 'In case you didn't know, they were held in Germany in 1936.' I couldn't help chuckling at their reaction.

"Of course, their attitude changed immediately, and they too time to enjoy looking at the pictures," Johanna added.

"Hard to believe," was Stephan's only comment.

Stephan was soon to have his own experience dealing with the FBI. Meanwhile, he was gathering his first impressions of America and Americans.

"Mutti, everyone is so well dressed here. Is everyone rich?" Stephan asked on their way to the grocery store.

"In some ways, mein lieber Sohn, (he liked it when she called him 'my dear son'), but not in the way you think. We have a great many comforts which seem like luxuries to most of the world…and in a way, they probably are. But we are rich in freedom, and we have inalienable rights, like it says in the constitution."

"You mean the Declaration of Independence," Arthur corrected her.

"Of course, the Declaration…"

"Wherever it means," Stephan interrupted, "I'm sure to like it."

When taking him grocery shopping, Stephan often shook his head in disbelieve at all he saw. This delighted both his parents.

"My God, all this meat and fresh vegetables and things. Lots of unbelievably great choices. Is this a special grocery store, or do the other places have such wonderful foods—and look at the candy. Please can I buy some?" His sweet tooth was always looking to be appeased.

"All right, but you are not to eat it so close to mealtime," Arthur said in his usual authoritarian voice.

"You must realize much of our food is rationed. We have food stamps," Johanna told him.

"Rationed? When there is so much?"

"Rationed so everyone can have a fair share, my son."

Stephan spent a pleasurable fifteen minutes deciding on what delectable confection he would chose while his parents finished the shopping.

Even though my parents lived in a basement apartment on Beacon Street, below the wealthy people for whom they worked, I was surprised at the comfortable lifestyle in which my family lived as housekeepers.

"I love how we can walk into town without being scared, and not be stopped by the police for identification papers. And the stores have so much…it's hard to believe…they have whatever one can possibly want. And there is money to buy things with," I babbled excitedly to my mother

"I guess working for a rather well-to-do family made me accustomed to shop for our employers in such fancy food stores," she told me.

That evening, over dinner of pot roasted meat and a heaping bowl of steamy mashed potatoes, my father told me, "You know, our employer, Mr. Block paid the $500 we needed to get you here."

"Yes," Mother added as she dabbed her lips with a white linen napkin, "he helped all of us. He's a good man. He remembers how his own parents were granted asylum in America. And I want you to know just because you help me do some work around the house doesn't mean it is a tradeoff for the help we received getting you here. Mr. Block will never tolerate that. You help me because you are part of our family."

"That sounds so good, 'part of our family,'" I said, still amazed at the riches I see around me.

"With all the food and other things, I don't think I'll have any trouble adjusting to America. After all, when one goes from nothing to something, it is extremely agreeable."

"I know, my son. I know," my father nodded in agreement.

I fitted into my new family life in no time and felt both totally comfortable and fortunate to have parents again.

When I lived in Chabannes, I never believed the lessons I had to learn in ORT of how to make things out of leather would ever come in handy. But it did. I managed to find work in Noymer's Leather Factory starting at forty cents an hour. Evidently, my training had been so good I got a ten and a half cents raise six weeks later.

After I had been living with my parents for about nine months, I had yet another close call with fate. There was a gas meter right over the headboard of my bed. One night a barely odorless gas had been seeping into my room. In the morning, when my mother called to me, I did not answer, so she came into my room, and noticed a slight odor of gas. She shook me, and when I didn't respond, she screamed for my father.

They told me later my eyelids seemed stuck together, and when my father noticed the gas odor also, he opened the bedroom window. I was unconscious, and they had to drag my dead weight from the room. They tried to arouse me by slapping me, but when that didn't work, they each took me by the arm and walked me around until I regained consciousness. Ironically, once more, I escaped with my life.

My father assumed the gas meter must be leaking and called the gas company. When Boston Edison Gas and Electric Company checked the box, they determined the leak was not coming from the box. Within an hour, the gas company ripped up the street attempting to locate the leak.

I got very nervous and upset when I saw the gas company trucks and what was being done. "I'm so sorry. I didn't mean to cause all this trouble," I told both my parents, thinking I was in some way responsible for the leak. "Whatever this is going to cost you, I promise, I will pay you back."

"They don't charge anything. You didn't cause this, and this isn't Germany," they told me.

Once more I had to shake my head in astonishment.

The phone seemed to ring at any time of day or night. People called Johanna for information, help, or just for a kind word of encouragement.

"It is amazing how many people ask you for help with their problems. Isn't it wearing on your nerves?" Stephan asked.

"Well, we received the kind of help we needed trying to find you, and it is only fitting we offer our help in return."

She was referring to acquaintances who were also refugees

attempting to locate a lost relative, especially a child, and living through the same agony as they had.

"We do whatever is necessary to bring that person or child over to the States, and we support each other.

"I've heard some of them say how very thankful they feel for the help you give them. You make me feel proud, Mutti.

"You know, aside from what you and Papa are doing, I think my first impression of Boston is the people and how lucky I am to finally be here."

Of course, both parents agreed.

Chapter Nineteen

About a month after he arrived he asked his father, "Papa, I just learned one of the boys from Chabannes lives in New York City. "Can I please go to visit him?"

"Do you realize what we had to do to take that 220 mile trip just to meet your ship."

"No. What did you have to do?"

"We are still considered citizens of an enemy country, so we had to plan traveling in advance. Not only that, we had to get a written character reference from two American born citizens and return those papers to the FBI."

"Well, how long does that take?"

"A long time when you are waiting," Johanna said.

Arthur continued. "It takes a week to process before they even send you a permit to travel anywhere, even a place as near as New York."

"They are very cautious," Johanna remarked.

"Then, when you fill in the travel permit, you will have to be precise about the time you want to remain away. Our time nearly ran out waiting for you."

"I have to give up my passport?" Stephan asked the clerk at the desk at the FBI office. He was more than a little nervous about giving up his precious passport as collateral. He knew if he ever wanted to extend his stay, he would have to submit another request which will take another week to process, making any additional stay impossible. Within twenty-four hours after coming back, he had to return the permit to the FBI at which time he retrieved his passport much to his relief.

Such was his life in the United States.

One evening, shortly after the dinner plates were cleared, Arthur invited Stephan to sit down in one of the living room chairs.

"I'm afraid I have some bad news."

"What can be so bad? Your health is all right, isn't it?"

"It's not that," he said, his voice quavering. "I just heard from someone in the IMAS there was a raid on Chabannes Castle. It happened after you left Marseilles."

Stephan paled when he realized, "God, I could have been there.

"By their behavior, the pro-German government of unoccupied France had demonstrated they willingly collaborate with the Nazis. In her very own words, Madam Argent told me on the very first day I arrived at her home, 'Be careful," she said. 'The officials and the police aid and abet their Nazi comrades all over 'Free France.'"

"Well," Arthur said, "the exception must be the French country folk around the area of the castle. They certainly do not have any use for the Germans."

"True," Stephan acknowledged. "They were generally friendly toward us boys and girls, especially because we kept to ourselves and weren't a nuisance."

"I found out that these particular villagers, along with the retired police chief, discovered, through the underground grapevine, the Gestapo had plans to raid the home, even though unoccupied France had not yet become totally absorbed by the Nazis."

"That figures," Stephan said.

"The mayor of the town must have told a small group of neighbors, including the retired chief of police, that they had to do something to save the children, so the chief volunteered. I can only guess what probably happened."

Arthur continued, "On the pretext of taking a stroll the night before the raid was to occur, the former police chief casually stopped by Chabannes, and warned those in charge of the children that the Germans were scheduled to come early the next morning on a raid."

"I remember him. He's a great old man. Good for him."

"The teachers then alerted the youngsters, warning them they had very little time, and to take only what they needed and to scatter immediately.

"Well, my son, I'm sorry to tell you some were not fast enough, and when the Gestapo arrived sooner than expected,. those who tried to escape by jumping out a window were caught and arrested.

"Some of the older boys, your age, sixteen and seventeen years old, managed to get away."

"All of them?"

"A couple of boys who were captured finally succeeded in escaping when they attempted it again. They then tried to sneak into Switzerland, but unfortunately, the Swiss border guards refused them entrance. Happily, they managed to find a flaw in the area where Swiss army lookouts were patrolling the border, and on their next attempt, they eluded the guards and made it safely into Switzerland."

Stephan learned later his friend, Henry, was picked up at Chabannes and was sent to a concentration camp. Happily, he survived. When they finally met in the Unitxed States years later, Henry told him the two others who did not escape died in the camp.

Sadly, all those who did not jump out of the window at Chabannes Castle were transported to a camp and were never heard from again.

In preparation for their immigration, Arthur had taken a course in how to operate a movie projector, believing this was a job in which he could work without having to speak English fluently.

"I've got to find something to earn more money where I don't have to do much talking. I am too old to become fluent in another language," Arthur told his wife and son.

While Stephan was attending high school at night struggling to learn English, Arthur, presently working as a butler, was attempting to master the mechanics necessary to become an American film projectionist.

Upon investigating what he needed to quality, he soon learned things in the States were considerably different from what he learned in Germany.

"In Germany, all I had to do was to flip a switch to run the projector. The electrical work was taken care of by calling in a specialist for the job. So, I was surprised at all they wanted from me, not like in Berlin," he complained to Johanna.

"What did you have to do, Papa?"

"In order to qualify for a projectionist's license, they put me in a large hall with many others. They gave me a tool kit, a reel of wire and a projection machine. I didn't know what the hell to do."

Regrettably, during his initial test, Arthur had a heart attack, probably caused by the pressure he was under, and he had to be hospitalized.

"Don't get so agitated," Johanna warned Arthur on a visit to the hospital. "You'll make yourself sicker."

"No, let me tell you so you know I'm no—"

She interrupted. "All right. All right. Tell me."

He continued. "Someone pointed to the wall. He told us, 'There's the electrical outlet. Now, get the projector connected and show the film.' And we had only so many hours to finish it. I struggled and struggled, and after about an hour, I got a terrible pain in my chest, and here I am." It took him a few months to recover.

Luckily, he passed the test the second time. That same day Arthur came home looking gloomy. "Well," he said to Johanna, "I got a job." He had been hired to work as an intern in the Broadway Theater.

"Why so somber?" she asked him.

"It's not a very nice place."

"Well, do they pay you? Then what do you care."

Stephan was listening intently when his father continued.

"It is as a film projectionist in…in…a movie house showing dirty movies."

There was dead silence. Then Johanna started to laugh. Soon the three of them were laughing. It was contagious.

"A dirty movie house?" Stephan said enthusiastically when he managed to take a breath from laughing.

"That's not so bad," Johanna giggled. "Who knows, maybe Stephan can go with you and learn a thing or two."

"Johanna!" Arthur shouted. "You should be ashamed of yourself."

Then he too burst out laughing.

Stephan always had free admission and used to go in the back door. At first he was fascinated with the arrangements the couples achieved. He wondered if he would be able to accomplish all those weird contortions. After seeing the same thing in other films, he grew bored and didn't go as often.

Father and son never discussed the films.

In all those years, in different orphanages, in different countries, away from my family, I learned to be stoic. Although I often times felt lost and panicky while others appeared calm, I kept my feelings inside, so I wouldn't appear vulnerable, and I took responsibility for myself. Now, at the ripe old age of seventeen, because of a little luck and my survival skills, I was happily in America.

My parents' employer offered me a job, but basically, since I had only an eighth grade education, I was limited both in schooling and in the English language. My father explained to Mr. Bloch that I was precise, methodical, and good with figures. It's extraordinary how well most parents know their children.

I confided to my father as we were going downtown to Federal Street, Boston, my new place of employment, "Papa, I am very nervous. I don't know anyone."

As he walked me to the elevator he teased, "Don't worry about it. They all go to the bathroom the same way, no matter how high up the ladder they are. But don't quote me on this."

The advise this fantasy created made me smile and removed most of the fear that was nagging me.

I walked into the office, and the manager spoke to me in English. I could feel the heat climbing up through my body to my face. My English was limited. I barely understood him. What am I going to do? The question went knocking around in my head.

I handled the situation as I did any other challenge. I toughed it out. I anchored my feelings on something deep down inside me so they couldn't escape. No one was going to know the fear I was experiencing. People who worked in the office had been prepared for my arrival by the controller, who was the department manager.

They all were very patient and kind to their new co-worker who barely spoke English.

"I love the job they have given me," I told my parents when I returned home from my first day at work. "I am absolutely fascinated with numbers. They're so...so...well...predictable. I think I would like working with numbers."

"That's wonderful," Johanna said.

"Papa, Mutti, I think I need some classes in English. I feel so ignorant...so limited. I want to be able to express myself better. Do you know what I mean?"

My father knew exactly what I meant.

"That's a splendid idea," Mutti told me, and my father agreed.

"You should continue to go to school nights, after work," he suggested.

And that is how I manage to start attending Boston English High School, grappling with English classes and other subjects I needed before trying to enter college.

After attending the first English class, I told my parents, "There were so many European immigrants in the class I didn't feel out of place. The only problem is we kind of slip back into our native languages when we are coming and going from other classes."

"You must insist on speaking English at all times. I know how hard it is to learn when one is older," my father reminded me.

It may seem like a little accomplishment, but it gave me such pleasure to be able to say in English, and face to face with my mother, "Mutti, the dinner was delicious."

Living with my parents felt perfectly wonderful and normal. I had a good year.

One night at dinner, celebrating my first anniversary in America, I reminded her, "Remember how you and I used to meet at the train station on my way to school when you were going to work? We exchanged my sandwiches for your delicious ones? You never told me how you managed to eat the ones you traded with me."

"Eat them? I didn't eat them," she told me smiling broadly. "I threw them away and ate a second sandwich I brought from home."

We all laughed.

Chapter Twenty

Times were good. In March 1943, when I celebrated my birthday with the people closest to me, I also registered for the draft which was compulsory. My father's health improved, and we were enjoying a good family life.

As fate would have it, though, I didn't have a chance to finish high school. I came home after my evening class to find an official looking envelope from the United States Government waiting for me.

"Greetings from the President of the United States. You have been selected…"

I was drafted.

I explained to my parents, "How ironic. I am going to br an enemy alien in the United States Army. It says here since I am an 'enemy alien,' the Army has given me three chances to decline their invitation to become a member of the armed forces."

"I'm just going to assume you are not considering turning down this invitation as you wished to turn down your visa in exchange for buying a bicycle," my father said with a serious look on his face.

"You're right. I do not think I want to refuse this offer. If I did, I know I could not become an American citizen. And, after all, Mutti, you did promise I would be a good soldier for America."

"And you will be, I am sure." Mutti told me.

One of the things I had to do was to certify that I had no living relatives in Germany. Because my birth mother's family denied my existence, I felt free to confirm "I have no existing family in Germany."

Finally, the day came when it was time to leave. I put a few necessary things together in my small suitcase, and both my parents went with me to the train station.

Going to the train reminded me of a different time, on a different occasion when we three had to go for a different purpose. I guess my parents also had this thought in mind.

"Take care of yourself," Mutti said trying to smile and failing.

"Write when you can," Papa said, almost like a command.

Mutti then slipped me a bag with my favorite cookies. "Here, a little something in case you get hungry."

"They will give you a leave after you finish basic training, I'm sure," Papa said, his voice tense.

And so, off I went to become an American soldier. What English I had not yet learned I was to learn in the Army, slang as well as words I would never use in front of my parents.

After my basic training in a medical corps at Rockford, Illinois, I was transferred to Camp Ritchie, Maryland.

My God, I thought. *I feel like I am back in Berlin.* I was now one of two thousands other German Jewish refugees serving in the U.S.Army. Also, I believe, among the Ritchie community were two hundred Native Americans, a situation which struck me as being most bizarre. I soon found out their purpose was to teach us draftees "army intelligence."

We had barely arrived at camp when we were all piled into a bus headed for Baltimore, Maryland.

"Hey, Sarge, where are we all going?" one of the passengers asked.

"You lucky sons-of-a-bitches are gonna become U.S. citizens."

Those of us who were not yet citizens were being transported up to Baltimore to take the oath that would make us genuine, real live Americans. The feeling of pride and triumph I had almost brought tears to my eyes. I thought of those bastard Nazis. I win, you bastards. Now, I'm gonna come and get you. Then I wrote to my folks to tell them the good news. "I am no longer stateless."

We finally got settled in, and I couldn't help remarking to my new buddy, "This place is really strange." With an exaggerated manner, in a heavy Berlin dialect, I said, "All ve guys in dees

American army uniforms, ve speak Anglish mit a wery European accent." We both enjoyed the irony.

Sometimes we tripped over what our European ears heard. One of the refugees, Heinz, from Washington Heights, was instructed to "Take the platoon in the morning and have the men fall into four rows with equal space between rows, one arm's length apart." This was a typical army formation. However, Heinz ordered us to "Fall in a column of bunches of four side by each."

Everyone turned in a different direction, and we commenced to bump into each other. Someone actually fell, which started us snickering, then chuckling, at which point we all laughed hysterically and couldn't stop. The laughter spread among those watching us, but what made things even more amusing was, in his confusion, Heinz didn't know what was happening. Of course, neither did we. Apparently, he did not have enough basic English nor basic military training.

Our schooling started at once. "Your mission will be to learn how to interrogate prisoners and make sense out of the information," our instructor's voice roared like a lion in heat.

At first I thought did he imagined we were deaf. It didn't take me long to realize most sergeants talk that way all of the time.

There was a Colonel Banfill in charge. He informed us Saturday night dances were held every eighth day. "By that, I mean, the war doesn't stop on Saturdays. At the end of seven work days, whatever day that is, that is when we will have a Saturday night dance."

We were not yet used to army ways. With very little explanation from our sergeant other than "This here book we managed to capture from the German army, identifies details of each German division." As we were handed a book called *Order of Battle,* the drill instructor continued barking more instructions. "You will pair off. One of you will give the facts from the book, and the other will ask questions. Your purpose is to obtain more information. Got that?"

"Yes, sir."

"Don't call me sir."

That is how we were drilled, learning to identify Germans and their divisions by their insignias. "Jesus, we have to memorize the history of every goddam German division, their fucking generals, their campaigns, the casualties they experienced, and even the firing power they have?" the boy in front of me asked as he turned around.

"Yeah. We have to be able to report on how much fighting experience and efficient leadership each division has."

"I feel like I'm back in school learning history."

He was right. It was a great history lesson.

One of our jobs was to spot the Native Americans who were running around at night in German and Italian uniforms, shooting off guns of various European armies. Our task was to detect them without getting "captured," identify their division, and by the sound of the guns, determine if the machine guns were German, Italian or Russian.

While in training, during a compass course exercise, one of the soldiers dressed in a German uniform, got turned around. Instead of heading for Camp Ritchie, he ended up at a farmer's house near Waynesboro, Pennsylvania, eight miles away. He had to ask the farmer for directions back to camp.

"I'm not really a Nazi," the man explained to the farmer. "I just got lost."

The farmer gave him the location of the camp without hesitation, at which point the soldier then rebuked him for being so trusting.

"Ya know, maybe you shouldn't be so quick to give a foreign soldier directions," the lost soul reprimanded the farmer.

"Don't worry soldier," the farmer snickered. "I ain't stupid. 'Round here we know you folks who play dress up in foreign uniforms are really Americans."

As we progressed in our training program, the complexity increased. We had to solve two different problems on two separate field exercises, one lasting 48 hours and another covering over seven days."

"This is going to be a bitch," my friend Gerd whined.

And he was right. On a week long maneuver we were taken into the mountains and dropped off at night in groups of four.

"Remember this compass reading. Now, get your asses in that direction," and our instructor pointed to his right.

We marched forward until we came to a tent.

"What the hell is that?" someone whispered.

"It's a tent, stupid," was the reply.

"Now what?" we asked the waiting Sergeant.

"Waddayathink you're supposed to do, have a party? Sit down and write all about your experiences trying to arrive here, and don't leave anything out," the soldier thundered. No one seemed to speak normally in this army.

After we did as we were told, we started to hike across country once more. Suddenly we were attacked by 200 hooting and hollering Native Americans dressed in German and Italian uniform.

"Jesus," the guy next to me gasped.

"What the hell?" I said.

To say we were startled and terrified is to put it mildly, but our job was to identify the "enemies'" insignias.

"What are we supposed to do?" said a confused participant.

"Identify everything. Do you know which army they're in?"

"I'm trying to figure out which division they belong to, and what their division background is. You figure out what the hell their casualty count is, and what guns they're shooting and whatever else we need to do."

As an afterthought someone said, "Jeez, I hope they are shooting blanks."

"Shuddup and write down whose guns they are."

"I think they are Italian."

"Sounds good to me."

When we completed our training, we were sent up north to Boston in preparation to board the ship which would take us overseas. The night before we were to go aboard we were treated to a movie in one of the dockside buildings.

"Hey, anybody know what the movie is tonight?"

"I think it's *Lassie Come Home*."

I was among the approximately 400 soldiers about to go to war coming out of the darkened theater with tears running down our faces, saddened over the fate of Lassie. I wonder what people would have thought if they saw us brave young men, who were about to be sent overseas to defend our country, crying like babies.

The next day someone reported, "Hey, we're going first class…on the Queen Mary, no less."

"Anyone know when we're leaving?" some anonymous voice asked as we were boarding the ship.

"What are you, an idiot?" our sergeant bellowed. "They can't tell us when we're leaving, you dumb ass. Remember security?"

"Oh, yeah. 'Cuse me Sarge."

After we boarded the ship, the powers that be decided we would not sail that night, which meant I had a chance to go home. My parents actually lived within walking distance from the dock.

My father knew what war was, having served as an ordinary foot soldier in the first World War. Both my parents tried not to show how anxious they were about what they believed could lay ahead for me, but I could tell they felt anxious by how much fuss they were making.

"Here, eat some more," Mutti suggested, as if I needed the encouragement.

"Are you sure you have everything you need?" my father asked.

"Maybe you should…"

And so it went.

I had to return to the ship around five in the morning. Both my parents got up before daylight.

"Here…some cookies I know you like," and she handed me a paper bag filled nearly to the top.

Mutti knew my fondness for sweets and must have saved rationed sugar for the cookies she made to give me. I don't know when she found the time to bake, but there were plenty of appetizing goodies to satisfy my sweet tooth. From the way my father was fighting back tears and looking grim, I suspect my father had a premonition this would be the last time we would be able to eat breakfast together. I also had to fight my emotions.

I returned to the ship, and that evening we received orders restricting us from leaving. We all knew this was a good indication we were about to sail.

My unit went overseas together. Ironically, among the passengers were about two hundred of us new Americans, refugees from Hitler's Nazi Germany. We so-called interpreters were now part of the US Army Intelligence Corp.

To avoid leaving a trail in the water for an enemy submarine to pick up, our ship maneuvered a zig zag course avoiding the sea lane.

"This fuckin' zig zagging is making me seasick," a new buddy told me.

"It's making me nervous, is what it's doin'," I answered. Those in charge, wanting to make us feel more at ease as we sailed, announced over the loud speaker, "This diversionary tactic is a safety precaution. Nothing to worry about soldiers. We're surrounded by our well equipped submarines, so we have plenty of protection."

"You don't believe that submarine story crap, do you?" one soldier asked of no one in particular.

"Yeah, like I believe in Santa Claus," some smart mouth snickered.

Of course, not one soldier believed the story. We just hoped the Queen Mary traveled faster than any submarine, especially German ones.

We arrived in England on D-Day, plus one. We learned the news of the invasion just before we landed, and we went wild with excitement. After we got our feet on English soil, we said our goodbyes to each other, were separated, and attached to several different divisions.

"Hey, where ya going, Steve?" my bunkmate asked.

"I've been attached as an interpreter to the Sixth Armored Division, Patton's Army. Where are you going, Charlie?"

"Great, so are Bernhard and I."

For about eight days we lived in the basement of a building in the

Chelsea section of London waiting to join our assigned units.

On one of our first nights here one of our buddies asked a British soldiers bunking with us, "What the hell is that noise?"

"It's one of those bloody buzz-bombs Jerry has been sending over Blighty."

"Don't start to worry" another added, "until you don't hear that noise."

"Yeah, when the noise stops, that bleedin' missile goes straight down and detonates instantly. Anyone in range of the explosion...well...good bye Charlie."

"Hey, my name is Charlie," Stephan's buddy said.

Now all of us were really scared. The idea that one of these bombs could actually kill us without defending ourselves blew my mind, so to speak.

"At least, if I have to face a soldier trying to kill me," I said, "I might have a chance to protect myself, but these damn buzz-bombs..." It was very, very frightening.

Because General Patton's army was not yet public knowledge, we were still in training without any shoulder patches to identify us.

"Remember, men, loose lips..."

"Sink ships. Yeah, we know," the young soldier responded, referring to the motto regarding talking gives the enemy information that can be harmful.

We felt as if there were spies all around us, and we knew any information we might inadvertently divulge would ultimately hurt us, so we traveled without any insignias or anything which could identify us as being part of the Third Army.

D-Day plus 10. After a beach head was established, we had our traveling orders and were transported across the channel. "I understand this crossing is remarkably smooth for this time of year," someone remarked.

"Oh yeah? That why am I about to heave my cookies over the side." And with that, he turned green and vomited as he predicted.

"Hey, what's the matter, Jack? You look green. Ha, ha."

Five minutes later the wise cracking soldier was hanging over the side, heaving his guts.

By the time we reached the French shore, we found a pontoon dock had already been built for us.

When we finally landed, we got the orders, "Take out your needle and thread at once, gentlemen, and proudly tack down on your sleeves the insignia of the Six Armored Division. You are now officially part of the Third Army."

Chapter Twenty-One

Stephan's unit started to march south, through Normandy, headed toward Paris.

"Wow," some unidentified voice yelled in excitement, "I"m going to Paree."

There was a loud cheer. "Wine and babes. What a war."

"Sorry, men. We are not going into Paris."

There was a widespread groan. "Ohhhh."

"Quiet, you numbskulls. It has been decided to give General DeGaulle and his fighting free French army the honor of taking the city whenever we get there."

The extreme frustration and great disappointment caused the air to turn blue with the number of expletives bouncing around.

Now it was the start of winter when they received new orders. "Your division along with another armored division will move north. Our objective is to open up the German encirclement around the American troops trapped there."

By the time the Germans attacked, the Americans in the Battle of the Bulge, Stephan's outfit had already worked its way to the southern part of Belgium.

"Hey, listen to this," the radio man told the men. "I just got word. When the Nazi Command demanded that General McAuliffe surrender, he answered, "Nuts!""

The men all let out a rousing cheer.

As they proceeded north, the vegetation grew denser, which limited the men's visibility. The extreme cold weather intensified. The winds were biting. The men shivered. Their teeth chattered. No amount of clothing kept them warm enough. The paradox was, whether from fear or struggling against the wind, they were sweating, making them even more miserable.

Snow was falling earlier than usual, adding to their difficulty. The trees, the mist, and the fog all added to extremely poor ground visibility. Allied air support was canceled. The few roads in the thick, lush, forest were narrow causing traffic jams on both sides of the front.

A major problem was created for both Armies. The only railroad coming into the area from Germany led to St. Vith, making it the most vital prize. After heavy fighting, it finally was recaptured by the Americans.

Stephan's outfit advanced. "Jesus, this whole village is destroyed," he told his lieutenant.

"Oh God, there are civilians laying frozen in the streets."

"Yeah. Have you looked in the barns?" someone asked.

"There are German soldiers stacked like cords of firewood in them like they're waiting for burial."

They found dead German soldiers in foxholes, their frozen feet stiffly sticking up in the air like a broken fence. Little did those American boys know the horrors they were seeing in these annihilated villages now would not desensitize them for the sights yet to come.

Endless delays as a result of difficult terrain, heavy snows, and the enemy diversion tactics, hindered the Ally attack.

"Jesus, can't have many more fuckin' obstacles if we're gonna win this fuckin' war," the shivering lieutenant complained, commenting on how the weather grew so cold the equipment started to freeze. The snow created an eerie blanket over the land making them easy targets of enemy rifle fire.

"God, what a sight," Stephan grumbled to Gerd as they crouched in their foxhole, doing all they could to do to keep from freezing.

Crack.

"Jesus, what was that?"

They were startled by the noise of a bullet whizzing overhead and ricocheting off a frozen growth in back of them.

"I'll find that sniping son-of-a-bitch and shoot a hole through him," one of the GIs in the next foxhole said.

Just then, another bullet flew over, but the marksman in the next hole fired immediately in the direction he thought the sniper was shooting. There was a scream and a stream of cries in German.

"Stephan, what the hell is he saying?"

"You got him in the balls. He's crying for his future."

There was a snicker. "That'll show you, you shit head." Anything to break the tension.

"Finish him off. I can't stand the screaming."

Another shot rang out, and the screaming stopped.

"Hey, ya hear the latest?" Lt. Cummings asked.

"Latest what?" Stephan asked shivering.

The lieutenant explained, "You guys thought it couldn't get worse? Well, listen to this." And Lt. Cummings started to read from the information he received over the radio. "Warn your men the Nazis are sending German soldiers dressed in American officers' uniforms across our lines. They speak perfect English without a trace of an accent. It is nearly impossible to identify them, especially from a distance."

"Oh...Oh," stammered Stephan along with several other interpreters.

"Wait, there's more." Cummings continued. "Be cautious of any direction signs. There are reports the Germans are turning them around so we head away from our destination."

"Ve betta be ver-r-y careful since ve speak mit wery heavy pronunciations, yah?" someone trying to ease the tension joked.

No one laughed. Everyone grew extremely nervous and more vigilant. Stephan, whose German accent was very conspicuous, started to feel exceptionally troubled about what was happening around him. Others, too, were on edge, and Stephan was feeling paranoid they might shoot an innocent bystander...HIM!

"All I need is a typical kid from New York or New Jersey associating me with one of the enemy. It would have disagreeable consequences to say the least," he told the intelligence officer who came from Toledo.

"Don't worry," someone joked. "With our accents, no one in his right mind would take us for the enemy. They are supposed to speak like us."

"I mean like us Americans."

"Not funny," was the reply.

"Stick close to me," Cummings advised Stephan.

"Don't worry. I will—like a bug on fly paper." And so saying, Stephan, more or less, "held hands" with his Lieutenant for three weeks. He wouldn't leave Cummings side for anything in the world.

"Hey, listen to this," Cummings told his men. "You won't believe the story I just heard."

"Try us."

"Well, when an MP stopped a general's car, the general was hopping mad. Evidently, this general had been stopped a few times on the road, and he was pretty irritated. He told the MP, 'The last time I was stopped they wanted to know the capital of Illinois. What do you want?'"

The MP wasn't phased at all. The guard apologized and told the general, "These hills are swarming with Nazis impersonating American generals."

"Okay, so what do you want to know?"

"Who's Betty Grable's husband?"

"How the hell do I know? I haven't gone to a movie in year."

His driver whispered, "Harry James."

"Harry James," the general answered.

"Good enough. Thank you, sir."

One afternoon, a few days after his outfit captured Breidfelt, Stephan and his buddy, Charlie, started to get hungry.

"The village looks secure enough. Lets find a little restaurant and grab some food," Charlie suggested. "Look, there's a place that looks like a possibility," looking across the street.

From the time he was sworn in as an American citizen, Stephan naturally had wanted to feel one hundred percent American, so he had trained himself to think like an American and do things the way he observed Americans do.

As he and Charlie were devouring their meal, Stephan looked over Charlie's shoulder and noticed an American officer sitting alone at the next table. This soldier never changed his knife from his right hand to replace it with his fork, as Stephan had learned to do when educating himself to eat like an American. Quietly, he got up from his table.

"Hey, whereyagoin?" Charlie asked with his mouth full of potato pancakes.

"Be right back."

Stephan approached a soldier wearing the insignia of the Military Police.

"That soldier over there is not an American," he told the policeman.

"Whadayamean?"

"He doesn't eat like an American, and…"

The MP interrupted, defensively, probably suspicious of a soldier dressed in an American uniform with a German accent. "Whadayamean 'eatin' like an American?'"

"Look, he never changes his fork from his left hand like we Americans. Remember, our officers warned us to be on the lookout for these kind of clues. I suspect he is probably one of those Nazi soldiers who pose as one of us. You might want to investigate. Better safe than sorry."

The six foot three American Military Policeman approached the soldier Stephan had pointed out. He engaged him in conversation for a few minutes when the MP forced the soldier to stand. Grabbing the suspect's arm, the MP pushed out of the restaurant, but not before the spy glared over at Stephan. Stephan returned his scowl with a sneer.

Stephan had been right.

Later, when he had to interrogate some of these spies, he learned the soldiers were tripped up when they agreed with deliberate inaccurate information such as referring to the Boston Red Sox great hitter, Ted Williams, as the greatest fielder of all times, or knowledge of the second chorus of the Star Spangled Banner. Hardly any red blooded American knew the words, but when a German was asked for the words, he would recite them verbatim.

The spy ploy quickly turned out to be less than successful, and much to Stephan's relief, the German army soon stopped this kind of tactic.

Stephan's outfit was currently enjoying a rest period.

"Lets wander around and see what we can see," Lou, Stephan's new buddy, suggested.

"Sure, why not. It's safe enough," Stephan agreed, "and it will give us something to take our minds off this friggin' cold.

They looked in several buildings and found nothing. Then another buddy yelled, "Hey, look what I found."

Lou and Stephan ran over to the warehouse across the street.

"Wow," the two late comers said.

"Jeez. Pickles!"

"Yeah, bunches of five gallon cans of sour pickles.

"Better yet. Lookee here." Stephan pointed to cases of Cointreau stacked neatly against the far wall. The men learned fast how to drink and enjoy the exquisite orange liqueur.

"Let's make room in the trailers for all this stuff," someone suggested. He received no resistance to the idea.

In order to take the delicious treasure with them, they must have thrown away half their equipment. They may not have dined on gourmet dinners, but to them, what they ate was extraordinarily palatable.

In the next village, roaming the streets, brought more good fortune.

"Wow, a brewery."

"For our self-preservation make sure the local brewery remains in good condition and the brew master is not taken prisoner," they agreed among themselves. They wanted insurance that they wouldn't be thirsty.

Stephan's division was on the march once more. They received new orders heading north again, ultimately crossing into Germany.

One night, shortly after entering Germany, they became aware that German soldiers were on either side of them. Evidently, their division headquarters had advanced so fast they were surrounded by Germans, instead of being in the middle of the American troops.

"This is weird," Robert whispered. "What the hell happened?"

"I dunno, but I think we even passed some of our own troops on the highway. They were supposed to be coming to save us."

"This fucking war sure is crazy."

"It sure is."

When they finally reached the French-German border, the men became extremely frustrated because they literally had run out of fuel in the tanks, in the jeeps, and in the trucks.

"Watch this," one of the men said as he started to drop a lighted match into one of the gas tanks.

Someone smashed the man's hand away. "Are you nuts?" someone cried as they all ducked. "The vapors are enough to blow us to hell."

"Shit, there ain't no vapors!"

Fortunately, he was right, and nothing happened. Lamentably, the tanks were bone dry. The supplies hadn't kept up with them. And the men were terrified.

"Jeez, if the Germans knew they had enough power to blow us all to hell in a counterattack, we wouldn't even have a chance to withdraw."

The next few days were very uncomfortable—everyone was on the alert. Happily, the supplies finally caught up with them.

"Where the fuck are we?" someone asked.

"I think we are somewhere south of Belgium," the young Lieutenant told the men. "Anyhow, we're further north than we were originally."

They barely entered Belgium when they received orders to change direction and now were headed straight for Germany. Stephan picked up a map of his division's moves, indicating every city they went through. He decided it would make a nice souvenir and put it in his pocket.

Chapter Twenty-Two

When they finally started up again, they crossed over the boundary into Germany and proceeded over the enemy's Siegfried line. Stephan and the others felt elated when they entered a deserted enemy bunker and found a complete telephone system.

"Look at this," I laughed. "Those smart ass methodical German son-of-a-bitches left an entire accurate map of all the telephones, bunker numbers and everything else they accumulated. It's all neatly laid out for us to read. What a find."

"Can we read it?"

"Sure." Then I said, "Watch this."

And over the intercom he called all the bunkers and informed the soldiers in them in his perfect German, "Kapitulation! Sie sind umgeben."

"What's he sayin'? What's he sayin'?" one of the non-German speaking boys asked.

"He's saying 'Give up, you're surrounded, you bastards.'"

The Americans outside the bunker heard a German officer screaming loudly at his men in one of the bunkers, "Nein, ÿbergeben Sie sich nicht. Nein, nein, nein."

"He's got the gal to tell his men '"No, no, no, you will not surrender.' The guy must be nuts."

They then heard a shot. Now, several German soldiers slowly crept through the door, hands raised in surrender. "Schieen Sie nicht. Wir ubergeben uns."

"They say they are coming out, guys. They surrender."

When Stephan and the others entered the bunker, they saw a dead German officer lying where he slid down against the wall, a bullet hole in his chest, blood staining the wall as he slid down from where he had been standing.

"You deserved it, you bastard," I snarled at the still bleeding corpse.

They tried to get the men in the next bunker to surrender but to no avail, so Stephan reported to his commanding officer. "This other bunker absolutely refuses to surrender."

"Get the army engineers over here right now. We don't have time to fool around with those friggin' idiots," the officer ordered.

A few minutes later two big, sturdy tall Americans, each carrying a heavy flame thrower appeared. Bringing up the rear were two smaller reproductions of the big guys. They were the ones walking nonchalantly behind. Their job was to "turn 'em on and burn 'em," one of them said. They pointed their flame throwers into the four openings of the bunker. The surrender was finally accomplished when the men from the bunker came out burning, their hair on fire. They were screaming. Their clothing was smoking. We watched horrified. Some of the guys vomited. The men who did the deed just shrugged their shoulders and walked away. The men who watched guessed they were used to it.

From that point on, they started to push forward, deeper into Germany. Their outfit was told, "You men are assigned to a position of great responsibility."

"What does that mean, do ya think?" a corporal asked.

"It probably means we are positioned directly on the front lines."

"Jesus, a guy could get killed."

"Don't joke about it."

The lieutenant explained, "Our job is to take as many live prisoners as we can and without delay."

The fighting was intense. They interrogated the prisoners as fast as they captured them.

"Now I realize just how practical our Camp Ritchie training experience was. It sure came in handy."

They managed to find out a great deal of important information.

"You cannot imagine how very satisfying this type of assignment is for me," Stephan told his buddy, Charlie, the company typist.

"What do you mean 'satisfying'?"

"When I have to question a prisoner I first confront him by deliberately identifying myself as 'Lavey,' in my most perfect Berlin accent; I enjoy seeing the surprise on the prisoner's faces when they hear how well I speak their language."

"But how does this satisfy you?"

"I'm coming to that. When these prisoners are questioned, some of them start to talk almost immediately; however, the captured officers, they are different, very different."

"Different how?"

"Oh, they start out quoting the Geneva Convention when we ask them certain questions."

"That's what they are trained to do, ain't it?"

"Sure, but I found a way to really convince those uncooperative bastard prisoners to talk. And I'm very convincing. When this arrogant SOB wouldn't talk, I took him to a deserted spot, and I told him very calmly, 'Here. Take this shovel. You don't have to tell me anything you don't want to, just do a little digging for us.' Then I instructed him ever so casually, 'Dig a nice, deep hole.'

"So, the prisoner reluctantly starts digging a hole, protesting all the while, yatita, yatita, yatita, whining, 'As officers...'

"Then I went right on as if he didn't say anything. 'Lay down and make sure you fit into it, I told him. I don't want you to be curled up or anything.'"

"I can hardly wait to hear what happened."

"Of course, the fucker then repeated the rules of the Geneva Convention quoting his name, rank, and serial number.

"I just acted very nonchalantly and continued to ignore him. I handed him two pieces of wood, and told him, 'Write your name, rank and serial number on this, so we can identify you at some future date.'

"Right after that, I had no trouble whatsoever with the interrogation. The officer answered all the questions I asked him.

"I tell you, Charlie, I love this job. Operating this way is my own personal vendetta. I probably could be court-martialed for my behavior, but I have an idea some of the commanders know what I'm doing and don't care as long as I get the info. Besides, some of them don't go by the book either."

"Hey, that's pretty good."

"As soon as I get the information I want, these Nazis are sent off to where the prisoners of war are imprisoned."

Subsequently, Stephan was surprised to discover that all this type of work was making him intensely aware of the bitter feelings he had swallowed and kept hidden deep inside, refusing to recognize. He carried these feelings with him through adulthood.

Later on, as our division continued fighting, we went through Frankfurt to Aschaffengurg. where we were assigned to occupy the place. Upon entering this city, for some reason, we saw it had not been bombed. We never found out why.

"Here we go again, boys," I said smiling when I saw the City Hall.

When we entered the building, we found all the police records just waiting for me to read. There, in typical precise German order, were the names of every person who held the position of block leader in the Nazi party. After I turned over these accounts and the information to my superior officers, I received the orders "Pick up these Nazis bastards and arrest them."

"With pleasure," I laughed. "This is one of the most gratifying jobs I have ever had during the entire time I was in the army."

I was soon given another assignment which gave me just as much gratification. Twice a week, on Tuesdays and Thursdays, I chose two of the largest, most muscularly built men from the Quartermaster Corps to accompany me, and then I appropriated a two and a half ton truck.

At four o'clock in the morning the three of us went knocking on the doors of people named on the list. When a door opened I asked, in perfect German, "Herr Whatsyourname?"

The man who answered the door replied, "Yah."

"You are to come with us." I gave no other explanation.

It was obvious our visit was anticipated. All the former block leaders were waiting for our call with a small suitcase already prepared. They said their goodbyes to their families. The two MPs grabbed the men on either side and shoved them, not gently, into the back of a truck.

I knew that seventy people could be transported in a two and a half ton truck with only enough standing room to carry a small bag. We packed these trucks full with 70 men, then drove the former block leaders to a collection point where we turned them over, along with their papers, to the next command. In the four or five weeks we were in this city, much to my delight, about several hundred prisoner were processed.

We had already heard about the concentration camps and the way the Nazis crammed their victims into freight cars marked 40 & 8, originally designed to house forty people or eight horses.

We had learned that the Nazis had crammed those cars full of people, with no toilet facilities and nowhere to sit, and delivered them to hell. I thought to myself these Nazi bastards are being transported in more civilized means of transportation than those railroad cars they are using to take Jews to the concentration camps.

Taking these men prisoners seems like the replay of the tragedy I remembered taking place when my father was taken away years before. I was especially pleased with this assignment, even though I knew the prisoners would not receive the same cruel treatment they had perpetrated on their fellow humans. It was my little bit of revenge.

When a German Major General was arrested, three GIs, including myself, took him back behind the front. We transported him in a tank so he couldn't be identified while being transported. This way we avoided being ambushed by the enemy in an attempt to rescue him. After we delivered him to the POW camp, we had to walk close to the cafeteria where the inmates were devouring fresh eggs, fresh meat, freshly baked bread. We lived on K-rations up in the front lines.

"They probably will get ice cream, too," I heard one of the GIs say, scowling.

These prisoners went to a detention camp where they had much better food than we, who were their victors. It was enough to make us GIs feel deeply demoralized.

Some of us Jewish soldiers were facing another battle within the United States Army which was most disheartening, that of overt or even subtle anti-Semitism. I was fortunate enough not to have met but one occurrence, and that was enough. I was working with an obnoxious non-Jewish Swiss-American sergeant who was two grades above me. I said or did something with which the sergeant disagreed.

"Well, that's the trouble with you goddamn Jews," he spit out his words at me.

I was so angry I wanted to takeout a gun and shoot him, but of course, I didn't. I couldn't. I felt the awful sense of frustration, of feeling rage, and worse, of being powerless.

Patton was the first American General to meet the Russians, and the other GIs and I were right there with him. We went well into Germany, which was far from easy, but finally we met the Russian army south of the city of Chemnitz where they stopped advancing.

Russian officers met the American army, and everybody celebrated. There was dancing and drinking...especially drinking. Everyone felt exuberant. All except Patton. He did not trust the Russians and did not shake hands with them. Later, I heard someone in the news media quote Patton as saying he wanted to continue on to Moscow.

I told my family later, when I was back in Boston, "I believe if Patton had been head of the army instead of Eisenhower, Berlin would never have been divided, and although the war might have lasted longer, we would have avoided a cold war. "To me," he told his parents, "Patton was a brilliant general."

Chapter Twenty-Three

It was April, 1945. Our division was the first of the American soldiers to come across a concentration camp, Buchenwald. The sight of half dead, tortured Germans, Russians, Poles, most of them Jews, angered and shocked us. The stench and appearance of walking skeletons overwhelmed us.

"What the hell," Lt. Cummings cried.

"Oh, Jesus," one of the GI's near me groaned. "There's a couple of fleece lined, United States Air Force leather jackets, lying around. There must be some Americans here."

We never found them.

When we saw the horrible conditions in the camp, some of us GIs got violently ill...vomited our guts out. I heard swearing like I never heard before. I saw grown men in our outfit crying like babies...sobbing out loud. One GI stood in the midst of all the squalor paralyzed, just shaking his head. I had, but did not show, a persistent sense of revulsion.

"Thank God you are here," a walking skeleton approached me speaking in Yiddish which I partially understood because it was so similar to German.

"A miracle I never thought I'd see," cried another starving soul, extending his bony hand in greeting.

It was an unbelievable sight. Skin hanging from the bones of starving, sick, barefooted people, their emaciated, cadaverous bodies barely covered in rags. They used their last bit of strength to approach us, crying, greeting us with their gratitude and thanks.

We didn't know what to do for them. We gave them some of our American rations. Unfortunately, we did not realize these rations were too rich for their undernourished systems. It made them sick.

They would require a different type of nutritional diet for the next few weeks or months before they could eat anything substantial.

My rage knew no limits as I saw the pile of human remains outside a crematorium. My muscles were so taut if someone came at me, I probably would have cracked like a china tea cup. At that moment, if a Nazi came within two feet of me, I swear, I would have killed him with my bare hands.

One of our officers discovered a pathology lab run by the SS. In it were pieces of tattooed skin taken from murdered prisoners, a lamp shade made of human skin and a couple of shrunken heads.

The experience was earth shaking. We were all emotionally affected. I for one will never forget it. Nor will anyone else who was here.

Every morning we drove into the nearby city of Stuttgart. Here we picked up two truck loads of elderly German men, who, probably, because of their age, were not in the fighting part of the war. We drove them back to the newly liberated camp to clean up all the human remains lying around.

"Ach du Lieber."

One unbelieving GI said, "They are crying, 'Oh, my God?,' like they didn't know what was happening here."

"Shit!" one of the veterans of the campaign shouted in anger.

"Vas ist los hier?"

"You can see what has happened here, can't you, you fuckin' Nazi?" another American yelled in the old man's face.

"God, they seem truly shocked. Their astonishment, their repulsion, their horror actually seem genuine," I said.

"We didn't know," some of them moaned.

I wondered how they could have denied how inhumane their fellow countrymen had been when the atrocities were conducted in their own back yard. The townspeople wanted to keep themselves safe by not acknowledging the truth. One of the things we learned in our training though was how to sense if someone were lying. The approximately one hundred men, coming everyday to pay penance in a way, did not have the faces of a liar. They were all truly disturbed.

"We knew there were prisoners being detained in this place, but I swear, we never... That was really all we knew."

As the man told me, he wiped the tears from his eyes. I believed him.

After a few days, word got around the city about the horrors of the camp. Over and over again I heard the people absolving themselves of responsibility by saying, "Ich wusste nicht. Wir wussten nicht." I wondered how could they have not have known just from the odors rising from the dead and dying.

"Der Geruch ist schrecklich," complaining that the smell was awful as they dragged the corpses to a burial pit.

I thought, *Breath deep, you bastards. It is you with your blind obedience to authority that has caused this.*

It was fascinating to observe the faces and the behavior of the townspeople and to hear what they were saying without them knowing I understood the language. I was pleased that to them I was just another typical American soldier.

For me, from the day we entered the camp, the past will always be present.

We learned later that about the time we were liberating Buchenwald, a brigade made up entirely of Jews, under the auspices of the British War Office, carrying their own flag, the Star of David, took part in the early stages of the Allies' final offensive in Italy. It was the first and only Jewish formation to fight in World War II under the Jewish flag, representing the Jewish people. Oh how I wished I and those damned Nazi brutes could have seen them.

We returned to the city of Aschaffenburg and were responsible for all the arrests made in the area. I'm sure when some of the residents heard we were entering people's homes and arresting them a few managed to escape.

One afternoon as I was walking down the city's street with another soldier, a woman approached us screaming in German, "Verhafte ihn. Vehafte diesen Mann." She was pointing to a well dressed civilian.

"Why should we arrest him What did he do?" I asked her.

We approached the man who seemed very nervous. He quickened his pace. In English, over his shoulder, he said in perfect English, "This woman is demented."

As politely as I could I told him in German to stop and wait on the spot until we questioned the woman further. He protested verbally, but he stopped walking.

"He is one of the Nazi military doctors in the concentration camp where I was. He experimented with chemicals on us inmates."

"How do you know that?"

"I was one of his victims," and she lifted her skirt and showed us her scarred legs. I winced at the horrible red welts.

"Sir, you are under arrest," I practically screamed. "We need time to investigate the charges."

At MP headquarters, when questioned, he denied everything, but while they were holding him, we decided to make our own inquiry in our own way. We asked him where he lived and then located the doctor's home. When we knocked on the door, his wife answered.

"We want to speak to you about your husband."

As we followed her into the kitchen, she started nervously wringing her hands and whining unintelligibly. She stood by the sink. Now her hands were shaking as she poured herself a glass of water. She acted as nervous as her husband. We laid two pistols on the table pointing toward the woman and asked, "Is your husband's name Dr. Salzmann?"

"Yah," she answered. "What is wrong?"

We ignored her question and proceeded to ask, "Was he a doctor in the camps, and did he perform experiments on prisoners?"

Shrugging her shoulders she protested, "I don't know. I don't know. I think so. Maybe. Yah."

That sealed the case. We left the wife to live with her conscience.

We prepared the necessary papers on him and the many other criminals we turned up who had committed atrocities. Then we shipped them off to allow somebody else do all the administrative work. We never found out what really happened to these prisoners later. I know I am a cynic, and that is why I would not be at all surprised if the U.S. Government brought the doctor and others like him to the States and gave him a fancy job with some government agency. After what has happened in my past, my distrust will remain with me until I die.

We were to be sent back home and discharged based on points. I had been through five campaigns, among which were the Normandy and the French campaign and the West and East German campaigns. We got one star for being in Europe and five stars, each worth five points, for each campaign. That gave me thirty points toward discharge. For every six months served in Europe we received a gold stripe, each worth five points. I was a staff sergeant which gave me four stripes and another point.

About this time I was among a dozen or so who received the Bronze Star for "outstanding service to our division." My lieutenant recommended me for the medal.

We were told to line up, and our division commander, a three star general, read the citation, "For heroic or meritorious achievement or service." He then pinned on the medal, and he shook our hands.

"Hey, we have ten points toward getting the hell out of Europe," we happily told each other.

Believe it or not, at the time, the bronze star meant nothing more to us than that. None of us recognized the medal for its value as an honor.

Today I acknowledge its significance, treasure it, and keep it safely at home.

It was now July, 1945, toward the end of this part of my service, when I received a letter from a family friend in the States. He informed me my father had a stroke. He was at home, confined to bed, in a coma. He failed to mention he died shortly before he mailed me the news.

The family had asked him not to tell me. They knew my father would not have been able to communicate with me if I had been sent home on emergency leave. They also believed the European war would soon be over, and feared if I were sent home I had a good chance of being shipped out again, this time to the Pacific. Survivors seem to have an instinct about how to avoid and overcome misfortune, and as survivors, they decided it would be best for me to receive the news after the fact and to stay where I was.

I soon received a second letter from the friend telling me the family had asked him not to tell me of my father's condition while he was still in a coma. He wrote more.

> Your mother sat on his bed and your father, seemingly unconscious, rubbed her arm. On occasion, when she left him for a few minutes your Aunt Maria sat next to him. He rubbed her arm once, then pushed it away. If it were not so sad it would have been comical. His eyes opened occasionally, but for the most part he remained comatose. He died peacefully about five days after the stroke. Your mother was at his side.

Now he was dead. And strangely, I felt absolutely nothing.

From 1932, when he placed me in the orphanage, until 1942 I did not live with him at home. We were separated once more after living together for only one year, when I shipped out to France as an American GI. The main regret I felt was I did not have any closure with him. I never knew, and now I would never know, how my father felt about anything. I know instinctively that he loved me and both my mothers. He loved neatness, his stamp collection, and astrology, but we never really had a chance to talk in regard to us—about him, about me—about life. He never knew I received the Bronze Star. I think it would have pleased him.

I thought about how my father brought me up. I guess some people might feel he didn't fit the pattern of a good and loving parent, and maybe he didn't, but at least now I can recognize how grateful I am that he was as strict with me as he was. Otherwise, I might not have been able to survive.

Once again our division was on the move. Because we were one of the first to arrive in Europe, it was decided to send us home, broken up into what they called armored battalions or small tank groups. It was planned to then ship us to the Pacific. We all felt tired, and none of us were the least bit enthusiastic about having to fight another kind of war in the Pacific, but we knew we had no choice. We were moved to one of the French ports where we boarded a troop ship.

"Now I know what a sardine feels like," I complained to the men in the two bunks directly above me.

"Ain't no Queen Mary," the one in the middle drawled.

"You should see the view from up here," our top bunkmate joked.

The odor emanating from crowded, unwashed bodies, made the trip most uncomfortable, especially considering what might lay ahead. We were sitting on the crowded deck, halfway across the Atlantic Ocean trying to breath clean air, when one of the men came running toward us all excited. "The news just came over the wireless. We dropped a bomb on Hiroshima, Japan."

"So what, we bombed the hell out of Germany."

"You don't understand. It was an atomic bomb."

"What the fuck is an atomic bomb?"

"I dunno, but the report said it wiped out the entire city—actually flattened the whole fuckin' place."

"One bomb? Jesus, Mary, and Joseph," the GI from Boston said reverently, almost under his breath as he crossed himself.

"I hope they blew a lot of those Japs to kingdom come."

No one cheered. Being unfamiliar with the atom bomb, we had no idea nor could we imagine the devastation it had caused—but to say it wiped out a whole city? All we knew was what destruction ordinary bombs produced, and that was enough. I guess we were all pretty sick of death and killing.

By the time we landed Stateside, a second bomb had been dropped on Nagasaki, and the war was over.

"Thank God we don't have to go to the Pacific and start all over again" was the comment heard throughout the ship almost prayer-like. We all agreed and felt particularly lucky.

The ship landed in New York, and we were sent up the Hudson River to an army camp. Here German war prisoners were assigned to wait on the tables, wash the dishes, and carry out all necessary routine work. When I arrived, we marched off the ship and headed straight for the long awaited and much appreciated hot showers.

"Okay, you guys," the Staff Sergeant drawled, "when y'all get cleaned up, get your asses over to the mess hall."

We finally were going to have our first authentic honest-to-goodness American meal. Oh, how the sight and smell of that gorgeous steak looked, surrounded by mounds of smooth white mashed potatoes. And fresh oranges! We hadn't eaten those for years.

As I was going through the line, the first thing I heard from the Jewish mess sergeant, who also cooked for us GIs overseas, was "You know, it's Yom Kippur today."

I knew Yom Kippur meant it was the Jewish holiday of fasting from sun down to sun down, but I just smiled and said, "Yup," and continued right down the food line.

As I sat down and started to eat, I overheard a German prisoner of war who was serving at the tables remark in German to another prisoner.

"This guy speaks with a German accent. He must be a stinking miserable Jew."

Now, needless to say, I had been looking forward to having some of that good old American food I dreamed about ever since I got on the ship to sail stateside—dishes I had not tasted for three years. This did not stop me, however, from taking my plate of food, a plate with all six compartments overflowing, standing up and shoving the dish right in the bastard German soldier's face.

He yelped, and then he gasped. It was good to hear. The Nazi POW may not have been physically hurt, but this arrogant German son-of-a-bitch's attitude disappeared as he wiped the mashed potatoes from his face.

To add insult to the German's injured pride, a loud hurrah emanated from all those in the cafeteria who saw the incident.

Needless to say, he was extremely embarrassed as he left the area, wiping his face with a napkin as the food dribbled down over his POW uniform.

"Don't know why you did that, buddy," someone said to me, "but I sure wish I had done it."

"Yeah. That SOB probably deserved it."

Shaking my head, I went back in line and got myself a new steak and more mashed potatoes. My little victory was bittersweet because I came to realize that my "war" was not yet over.

Nobody objected to my behavior, and nobody referred the Geneva Convention. I knew I probably could have been brought up on charges, but I wasn't, and I most likely wouldn't have cared.

A few days later, from New York, the army shipped me to Camp Campbell, Kentucky, an armored forces camp. Here they processed my discharge papers.

"Kinda crazy sending me all the way from New York to Kentucky when New York is so near to Boston," I told one of the men being discharged with me.

"I know. It's the army way. I'm headed back to New York myself."

Chapter Twenty-Four

His homecoming was tearfully sad and joyous at the same time. "It's great to be home again," he told his mother, as he hugged her, and she kissed him soundly on both cheeks. He showed her the souvenirs he had collected and gingerly opened the box holding his Bronze Star.

"Oh, I am so proud," Johanna said.

"I kept your promise. I was a pretty good soldier."

"I knew that was the only type of soldier you could be."

"I just wish Papa could have lived to see me home."

"I know, my dear. He would have been very proud too."

"I don't know. I just never seemed to be able to please him."

"I doubt that."

"That's because you met him when I was no longer living at home. He could be very severe and often times he was."

"I find that hard to believe. He never showed me that side of him."

"Maybe it's because...well, you were instrumental in melting away that part of him. God knows, my birth mother witnessed a great deal of how he treated me, and she never even tried to stop him. I think she was afraid because, I swear, when he hit me with the back of a knife, I recognized a look of pain on her face as young as I was."

"He hit you with...?" Johanna's mouth fell open. "Well, that is all in the past now, and there is nothing anyone can do to fix the past—we can only correct the present. And I love you enough for the both of us."

"I love you too, Mutti," Stephan said, and he threw his arms around Johanna, squeezed her, and kissed her cheek.

For me, being home meant sleeping late, eating leisurely breakfasts, and talking endlessly with Johanna. We both enjoyed each other's company.

I would take short walks around the city, and when I came home, Johanna was already home preparing dinner. One day, after one of those walks, I went into the living room, and in the corner of my eye, I saw what appeared to be an official looking envelope lying among the rest of the mail on the dining room table. I picked it up and saw it was addressed to me from the State of Massachusetts. I can't be drafted again, can I? I thought a I nervously tore it open. "Wow," I yelled. "Mutti, guess what!"

"What are you yelling about?"

"I just received a notice that the State of Massachusetts is giving its veterans a bonus of $300 for having served in the army."

"You know, Hasekin," my mother said smiling a broad smile. "You earned every penny for having done such a great job."

Digging my fork into a delicious serving of pot roasted meat, I grinned back at her, nodded me head, and said, "I agree with you one hundred percent."

One of the first things I did to test my new found freedom was to take a train to New York to visit friends. Wearing a pin, affectionately called by many as "the ruptured duck," signifying I was a veteran, I displayed it prominently on my lapel. I remember snickering to myself, "Now I don't have to get the FBI's permission, or anyone else's permission to visit my friends. I'm gonna drop in to see Henry and Ruth just because I can."

We had lots to celebrate and reminisce about since we had been together in the French orphanage.

"Remember the time we nearly got shot creeping into the fields to find food…any food?

"Yeh, and how we sliced turnips and stuck them to the stove and…?"

"You couldn't get me to eat turnips today if I were starving."

"And the time you left your bicycle under the window and…"
And so it went.

On the train ride back to Boston, perhaps because we had been discussing survival, I started to think about my grandmother.
The last address I have for her is now in East Berlin, I thought, *but maybe it will still be good. I wonder what her reaction would be if I contacted her. One thing sure…I won't try to contact any other of my birth mother's family.*

When I arrived home, I wrote to the only address I knew—Alt Glienicke—the place where my birth mother grew up.

"The reason I want to write," I told Johanna, "is because I want to contribute towards repurchasing my birth mother's grave site."

"I can understand that," Johanna said.

Weeks later I received a reply. I held the envelope just looking at it at first, hesitating to open it.

"I imagine you are a bit nervous about the contents, but if she answered you, it surely is a good sign."

I looked up at my understanding mother, and I managed a slight smile of confidence before I tore open the envelope.

I started to read. "Listen to this," I said to Johanna. "This part is interesting. Listen." And I read from my grandmother's letter.

"'I am sorry I had to behave as I did, Stephan, but we were all terribly afraid. Our neighbors were turning in their neighbors for the slightest infraction. We didn't know what to do about you. We were also afraid you could get in trouble.'"

"It must have broken her heart not to get to know you."

"She also discourages me about the grave site because the cemetery is slated to be eliminated to make room for an Autobahn. It's really weird."

"What do you mean, 'weird'?"

"She reminded me that in Germany graves in Christian cemeteries are not owned in perpetuity like the graves of Jews."

"Oh, that must make you feel terrible."

"She confirms that it is customary for a plot to be repurchased every twenty-five years, or it is abandoned to be used for another burial, and an extension has not been paid for."

"I guess that is why the Jewish community members were assessed higher taxes put upon us," Johanna said.

"At least I'm glad I remember the good times we had together, even if they were short-lived, but then to learn about this...this desecration...well..."

And like his father used to do, he left his sentence unfinished.

From the time he learned the road leading to the airport in Berlin was to be built over the grave of his mother, he refused to fly directly into Berlin. Years later, the German government offered Stephan the opportunity to visit the city of his birth as a former resident. To avoid driving over the place where his mother had been interred, he and his wife flew into another city and took the train to Berlin.

Stephan had been home a few months when his mother decided, "Stephan, it is time to move on. This apartment is a constant reminder of sad memories of your father's illness. I miss him terribly, but I think you and I have to get on with our own lives."

She quit her job as housekeeper and got another job as a bookkeeper almost immediately. During the post-World War II era, apartments were in short supply because of all the veterans coming home, marrying and setting up housekeeping. To rent an apartment, landlords had to be bribed. This way the owners could get a hefty fee, tax free.

"If you want the apartment, Mrs. Lewy, you know, you gotta pay a little 'under the table' so to speak."

"How much under the table?" Johanna asked, referring to the bribe the landlord suggested.

"It'll cost you $300 to move in."

So, in 1947 they found a suitable place at 14 Center Street, Cambridge. The building into which they moved might as well have been in the center of Europe. In fact, the sixteen apartments in the building were owned by a Russian woman who didn't speak any English. They were occupied by mostly German and Austrian Jewish refugees. They could speak to each other in their native tongue which was easier for them and made them feel more comfortable.

Even though Stephan's English was now perfect, and he and Johanna spoke it at home, English was not needed nor spoken in the entire building. The odors of familiar foods and sharing little tastes of each other's cooking seemed to ease the agony many of these families felt after having lost loved ones who had been left behind in Europe and had perished in Hitler's concentration camps.

Veterans, if they chose, had the privilege of going back to the jobs they held before they left for the service. Stephan went back to working for his previous boss.. His employers soon realized how good he was with figures and assigned him to work in the accounting department.

Johanna was a wonderful, loving, nurturing parent, so unlike his father. She wanted the best for Stephan, no matter what his goal might be. "The only way to do this is by receiving a good education," she told him at every opportunity.

I had always dreamed of going to college, and the United States government gave me that chance when they created the GI Bill of Rights.

I told my mother, "the greatest thing in the history of the world occurred when the United States government created the GI Bill of Rights. I can go to school, and the GI Bill will pay for my tuition, my books and a small stipend for living expenses."

I needed to finish high school before being admitted to any college, so I enrolled in Lincoln Preparatory School, an affiliate of Northeastern University, where I planned to apply. It was an accredited university and has an excellent reputation.

I received credit for math and languages. I took the required courses of English, American history, and finally became eligible to enroll in the college of my choice. Naturally, I chose mostly business courses, concentrating on those subjects which would help me advance in my chosen field, accounting.

Finances were tight. On some weekends the only entertainment I could afford was the free dances offered by the Immigrant Mutual Aid Society in a hall hired for the occasion. Here refugees would have coffee and cake on a Saturday night, and here is where their young adult children met other young adults.

"Gunther, it's good to see you again," I said when I met my cousin after years of separation.

"Goin' to school huh?"

"Yes, Northeastern University. It's great."

"School is not for me, even with the GI Bill. I want to go into business and earn big bucks right now…maybe open a dry cleaning store."

We never had been very close, and even now our different attitudes contributed to our relationship remaining somewhat distant.

At these socials my mother proudly introduced me to her acquaintances and their children. I was greeted with "Ah, we've heard so much about you" and "We were beginning to believe you were a figment of your mother's imagination."

It was a place where I could and did make friends in spite of my reserve.

"At least we are all in the same financial position," Stephan whispered to his new friend, Ernie.

"You can count on that," Ernie added.

Many of our activities were at the mercy of the small monthly benefit of the GI Bill. Most of the young men were ex-GIs, and when we had dates, we met with them in our homes to chat over coffee and share our war and school experiences. Meeting in each others houses seemed to be the only way to socialize.

I loved the movies, so when I had some extra money, I went to the Astor Theater on Tremont Street, the first movie house in the area to have reclining seats and a larger than normal screen.

Always cognizant of finances, I told my mother, "I sure hope the Astor will make a go of it. They had to raise the ticket price to 65 cents."

In Boston, I was able to take advantage of free outdoor concerts presented by the Boston Pops held every night on the banks of the

Charles River during the month of July.

On Sundays, for the price of a couple of cups of coffee, friends and I attended really good jazz concerts in one of the few coffee houses where jazz groups entertained.

"I remember when I was living in an orphanage they had only one music evening a week, on Wednesday nights. We listened to classical music on 78 RPM phonograph records and discussed composers and their backgrounds," I told one of my friends during intermission. "Quite a difference from what I can do now."

In 1946 Stephan met a charming European girl, Gloria. They liked each other and soon started going together exclusively. Evidently her parents thought their daughter had at last found an acceptable husband, and they started pressuring Stephan.

"So, when do you think you two will get married?" the girl's father asked Stephan as they waited for the maid to bring in dessert.

"Papa, please…"

"Well, I'm interested in Stephan's intentions."

Stephan picked up the coffee spoon and stirred his cup a bit too vigorously, splashing dark brown spots on the immaculate white linen tablecloth.

"Oh, I'm so sorry."

"That's all right, now about your intentions."

"I think marriage is fine, but I don't think it's such a good idea for Gloria and me to get married right now," he told her parents.

"Papa, please!" Gloria interrupted again, squirming with embarrassment and looked to her mother for assistance which was not forthcoming.

Stephan started to feel manipulated, "I'm really not ready to make such a lifelong commitment."

"If it's money…"

"Papa. Stop!"

"No, not that."

"Well, there's no reason to wait," her father said. "And if you need help, we can afford it."

The family's frustration was mounting as their attempts to control and manipulate Stephan's future made his survival mode send rockets soaring.

"It's really not a good time," he told his girlfriend's father.

"Well, in that case, I want you to stop wasting my daughter's time."

Gloria left the room abruptly.

Stephan lost his first girlfriend.

Chapter Twenty-Five

When I smell something familiar, like the odor of cookies when they first come out of the oven, or when I eat food that reminds me of something that occurred in years past, I can close my eyes and fondly recall seeing a group of German refugees sitting around a cozy living room enjoying their Sunday afternoon old world tradition of meeting socially in each other's homes.

We, as adult children, were expected to make an appearance at these weekly coffee latches. Here the older folks, speaking easily in their native language, discussed things in general and the uniqueness of their children in particular.

Very little was expressed about their former lives or the suffering they endured. America was now their home, although they still held on to some of their old traditions and still carried their formal European social habits with them. I remember this particular incident at my mother's house that reminded me how the past is always present.

"You know," my mother told Ludwig Herzberg, "I have fond memories of you when we met in Berlin."

Then Johanna turned to one of her guests and explained, "The Herzbergs came to the States with their two sons, in April of 1939, shortly before we arrived. Now, since both families settled in Boston, we see each other socially."

"We have become great friends, as did our sons, Ernie and Stephan," Johanna said.

Mr. Herzberg had a very heavy German accent which, in spite of his European experience as a successful business man, kept him from acquiring a suitable position befitting his background. He found employment in a factory, working on a machine, which allowed him to avoid unnecessary conversation. This situation was the downside for many European refugees.

While I was enjoying my favorite butter cookies on this particular Sunday, I heard what I consider a delightful discussion between my mother and Mr. Herzberg, reminding me how very European my mother's friends remained.

"I do remember meeting you in my sister's office in Berlin, how many years ago?" Mr. Herzberg reminded Mutti as he raised his coffee cup to his mouth.

"Many, many years ago," Mutti said.

"And now in the United States?"

"At least fifteen years," she answered with a puzzled look. "Why do you ask?"

Mr. Herzberg put his cup down on the coffee table and said to her, "I think we have known each other long enough so we can address each other using the familiar 'du,' rather than the more formal "sie," after all this time."

No one laughed. This was serious business.

"What does Mr. Herzberg mean by the word 'du?'" one of my non-German friends quietly asked me.

I explained that 'du' is the familiar form for 'you' and is used only among very good and close friends.

It took another ten years, twenty-five years all together before they started calling each other by their first names.

Yes, indeed, social habits die hard.

In the forties many of us young adult sons and daughters lived with our parents, usually until we married. In spite of what we veterans saw and experienced, it was still the age of innocence. We didn't go to bars to meet potential dates. We were not that sophisticated, nor did we have the money.

What did we do? A cheap way for young adults to meet was to go to the various dances sponsored by churches and synagogues around town. My cousin Gunther, my friend Ernst, and I decided to go to a Jewish single dance held in a hall at Coolidge Corner, a popular shopping area in Brookline. Here we were hoping to meet some nice girls. On one of these occasions, as we three young men were watching others dance, an attractive young lady passed by in front of my two friends and approached me.

"Wanna to dance?"

"Didn't I see you with someone all evening?" I asked.

"Oh, you noticed. Well, yeah. We're just leaving. He went to get our coats, so we have time for a dance if you want."

Suddenly my shyness seemed to dissolve. "Sure, why not?"

"Want my phone number?" she asked me while we were dancing.

"I…I guess so," I stammered cautiously. She caught me off guard.

"By the way, my name is Frances."

What fascinated me about this attractive young woman was how straightforward she was. I offered her my pen. She took a piece of paper from her purse, and she wrote down her telephone number.

I was ready to throw caution to the wind. I liked this girl immediately, in spite of feeling somewhat apprehensive because of my recent past experience. I figured if I stayed vigilant I'd be all right. I gathered my courage and called her a few days later.

"I am utterly fascinated with this girl's eating habits," I told Ernst after Frances and I had our first date. "It seems as a child she was quite chubby, and now, in order to control her weight, all she eats is sauerkraut and drinks nothing but coffee."

"Wow," Ernie said, encouraging me, "Besides being attractive and nice, she's an uncommonly cheap date!"

After dating Fran for a few weeks, I urged her to eat normally. "You look just wonderful to me."

I invited her to our apartment for dinner. I guess I really wanted my mother's approval. Mutti had good instincts. Not to worry. Frances and Mutti clicked right away."

Mutti realized my relationship with Frances was serious long before I did. She invited Frances to come to dinner the following week and invited my Aunt Mimi, Gunther's mother. Mimi was not at all accepting. After dinner, over coffee, Mimi hardly stopped for breath between her probing questions.

"What kind of schooling do have you?

"Mimi, your voice sounds harsh," I interrupted, trying to soften what I saw was happening and about to happen.

"We should know more before you get too serious. Now, what about your father? What is his background?"

"Mimi, please." I could see Frances clenching her jaw.

"This is important. Is he a professional man? What university did he attend?"

I kept interrupting Maria to no avail. My mother tried several times to change the subject, and after a few uncomfortable moments, she succeeded.

"Let's give the child a chance to know us too," Mutti said to her sister, referring to Frances. "Now, who's for more coffee?"

Even though I knew Mimi was being very Germanic inquiring about my American girlfriend's family, I deeply resented her attitude. She behaved like a battleship in a battle with a frigate, "damn the torpedoes, full speed ahead," acting as if Fran was the antagonist.

Frances, an all American girl, unaccustomed to this type of treatment and not knowing what to make of such an interrogating interchange, answered as calmly as she could under the circumstances.

Apparently Mimi had made up her mind. "You must consider," she told Mutti and me later, "the fact is, this girl's family does not rise to a high enough standard for you, Stephan."

"Don't you think that is for me to judge?" I asked trying to hold back my anger.

"The trouble with your girlfriend, Stephan, is nothing is too good for her. She always wants something better," Mimi spat out her displeasure, as if Frances had committed a crime.

Trying to alleviate this awkward situation, I replied, "Well, she's got me, and she can't do any better than that."

Mimi scowled. Her criticism of Frances meant nothing to me, but it put a distance between the two of them which remained for years.

Mutti, on the other hand, never questioned Fran. She respected my feelings, asked nothing, was nonjudgmental and accepting.

We were celebrating New Years Eve with our friends at a small party when Fran said to me, "Tomorrow starts a leap year, and since you haven't said anything, it's a woman's prerogative to propose on New Year's Day, and I am going to propose to you."

"You know I'm still in school and..."

"I don't care. I have a job, and you have the GI Bill."

"Fran, I love you very much, but I guess I'm old fashioned enough to want to support you without you having to work."

That was mostly the norm in those times, but we were in love, and emotions sometimes override logic.

I told my bride to be, "You realize if we get married now, we will have to share an apartment with either your parents or mine."

We didn't have to ask. My thoughtful mother stepped in. "Listen, you two. I know apartments are scarce with so many of you GI's marrying and needing places to live. I have room, so if you think it is okay, you can share my apartment."

Since Frances's parents still had a young son living at home and Mutti's place was larger, we happily accepted her offer.

We were married in September of 1949 while I was still in school. To help out financially, Frances worked days and attended Chamberlain Junior College at night.

During the next three years, while attending night school, time and money limited our social life as it did with all our friends.

One day when I came home from work Johanna greeted me with some good news.

"A while ago, the German government offered former citizens who had suffered excessive hardships under the Nazi regime what they call reparation."

"Excessive hardships! Those Nazi bastards put a fancy name on the degradation they put us through. What are they doing? Trying to ease their consciences?"

"Probably. But if they are willing to pay, I figured it wouldn't hurt to apply to the German government for reparation in settlement for how your father's business was practically stolen by one of those Nazis. Since, to use their term, it had been confiscated and he was prevented from earning a living, as his wife I was qualified to receive some money. And," she said, waving an envelope in front of my face, "Here it is!"

"That's great, Mutti. I'm glad for you. I guess they are working hard trying to ease their guilt."

"Be that as it may, what is even more befitting, I also applied for you. You were eligible for having had to delay your education for over five years. The money will come in handy for you and Fran."

"Thanks for thinking of me. I'm not that bitter that I won't take the money they owe me."

I kept my job working for a mining company for the next five years while attending school three nights a week.

"I finally did it," I said to Fran when I got my final grades. 1953 is a great year to remember, the year I earned my Bachelor's Degree in Business Administration. "I feel terrific."

"And to think," Fran said, "You graduated with a GPA of nearly 90% and as a member of an honors fraternity. I'm so proud I could bust!"

"Not bad for a kid who couldn't speak English only a few short years ago," I told my two female admirers.

Many years later, when I observed my own children studying several liberal arts courses, I realized there were many gaps in my formal education. As a parent, I saw my children doing their homework and recognized how much more they benefitted from their academic education than I had. Watching each of my children as they approached seventeen, I recognized how much more mature I had been at that age. I also recognized the huge differences between them and me academically.

In a way it saddens me at how much I missed growing up, and I sensed a feeling of inadequacy in myself. I acknowledge how their distinct experiences made such a difference in their development in contrast to mine, but I never was able to tell them how I feel.

Chapter Twenty-Six

After graduation we told my mother my company was sending me to their Salt Lake City office were I had a good job waiting for me as an accountant. We are moving.

"Before you two move, I think your father would feel now is the appropriate time for me to tell you the results of the astrological family studies he calculated."

Fran and I looked incredulous, and my mouth fell open as Mutti revealed the accuracy of his findings.

"He knew your birth mother would die at a young age, that he, your father would cross a large body of water and he would not live beyond the age of 52."

Coincidence? I don't think so. I felt stunned. I only wish he could have figured what was in front of me...of us, but it wasn't to be.

Our move to Utah proved to be successful financially and socially. "Fran, I'm sorry I have to travel so much, but the job calls for it."

"Don't worry about me, Shtefan," calling me by her pet name. I'll be fine."

Unlike the man she married, Fran's outgoing personality helped to make many good friends while I was on the road.

After living in Salt Lake City for only a short time, Fran had a miscarriage, much to our great sorrow. I was away at the time, but the wonderful friends she made gave her the support I could not give her. I received the news while on one of my trips to Alaska. In my hotel room I sat down on the bed heartbroken. At first reading the letter, I must have been in shock. Then, all of a sudden I started to cry, just tears at first, then the dam burst. I don't remember when I ever cried. Now, I cried for my wife. I cried for all the people who had died at another's hand. I cried for all the times I didn't allow myself to cry.

While in Salt Lake City, I took the Massachusetts CPA exam and was lucky enough to pass it the first time. "Fran, I will have to change jobs. I have to find work for three years with a Certified Public Accounting office to fulfill the requirements." Fortunately, I received an offer for an excellent position as an accountant back in Boston.

"I'll be sad to leave the wonderful new friends we have made, but the alternative is 'T-riffic,'" Fran shouted when I told her the news. "We'll return to our old friends and family, and that ain't bad."

Once again, fortune smiled on me. After completing the required time, my position led to another excellent job with a large hotel chain in Boston.

A few months after our move back to Massachusetts, Fran became pregnant again.

Toward the end of the pregnancy, Fran's doctor said it was best to induce labor. I don't know why, but as I drove her to the hospital that evening that suggestion made me very anxious.

"Don't worry, Shtefan," using her pet name for me. "Go home and get a good night's sleep, probably the last one until our baby leaves the nest," she said smiling. "I won't have the baby until the doctor comes tomorrow morning."

I kissed her goodbye, then returned to our apartment. As hard as I tried, I couldn't sleep. My imagination was driving me crazy with "what ifs." I got back to the hospital very early the next morning. I did not want to miss anything. As fate would have it, I fell asleep in the waiting room and was awakened by the doctor smiling down on me.

"It's a boy, a hungry big eight pound 14 oz bundle of enthusiastic energy," he told me. And so in November of 1955 our son was born. We named him Arthur, after my father.

It was great to be surrounded by a loving family. Three years later our lovely daughter, Ellen was born. Needless to say, our mothers doted on their grandchildren. For me, during the day, life seemed rewarding, but I was always waiting for the other shoe to fall.

At night my dreams haunted me. My experiences from my past

seemed to affect me still. I held tight to the two people on whom I could count, my wife who sat up with me nights until I could shake my nightmares, and my mother, who supplied the maternal love I missed growing up. The thought they were nearby steadied me.

In 1964 the other shoe finally fell. My mother, who had remarried the kind and gentle Morris Smith, widower of her friend Lil, had a stroke which left her completely paralyzed for months. We were all shattered. I wouldn't allow myself to consider the possibility she was going to die.

I visited her daily, sometimes twice a day. I felt stupid asking her "How do you feel, Mutti?" I didn't know what else to say. My feelings were locked away in an impenetrable vault, hidden deep down somewhere inside of me. I wanted to thank her for teaching me how to love and to be loved. I wanted to tell her how much I loved her. But all I could say was "How do you feel?" and feebly try to encourage her to get well. I could not picture my life without her.

I finally was able to tell her, "Morris and I are looking for a exceptional place for you to recover and get physical therapy. Only the best for you, Mutti."

She would smile, and her eyes would tear, and she whispered, "Thank you, Hasekin."

With good professional care and training, she was able to return home to her beloved Morris and those who loved her. Although she now learned to do things around her apartment, she could not work professionally outside the home. The lack of independence annoyed her, and in a self deprecating way, she teased us about it. "Who would want a half paralyzed bookkeeper?" she joked.

A year and a half went by. My immediate family was healthy and happy, and my mother seemed to be content. She had her appetite back. She was able to make coffee with a little help from her devoted Morris, and she enjoyed seeing the many friends who visited her. "Sorry, I can no longer make baked goods, but these cookies we bought seem even better than mine, right Stephan?"

I always answered, "No. Not as good as yours, Mutti." She would smile at me and made me feel all was well.

One Sunday when we were all visiting Mutti I noticed she had developed a bad cough. "You shouldn't be smoking with a cough like that," I told her.

"I keep telling her," Morris agreed, "but she never listens to me. She always says she's too old to quit now. 'Besides,' she says, 'what else could happen to me?'"

We finally convinced her to go to the doctor. He recommended a chest X-ray. It came back positive for cancer.

Soon after the diagnosis, her racking cough got worse, and she was hospitalized once more, sedated against the ravages of pain that took over her body.

"I hate being so groggy," she told us.

"Well, it's better than suffering," Morris told her lovingly.

We all agreed.

"You know what I mind most, Hasekin, about dying..."

"Don't talk like that," I almost yelled choking on the words.

"Stephan...be real," she murmured. "I started to say..."and a racking coughing spell slowed her from finishing, but only for a moment "...you know what I mind most about dying? It's not being well enough to go to my wonderful grandson Arthur's bar mitzvaht. Remember yours, Stephan?"

"Oh, yes," I said as I tried to hide my tears. "I requested corned beef and cabbage for the party meal. I remember."

She continued to reminisce. "And do you remember that SS man waiting for us at the top of the stairs?"

"I sure do."

"Oh yes. Well, thank God, Arthur's bar mitzvah will be different."

In the autumn of 1966, six weeks after the diagnosis, she took her last gasping breath. Fran and I were inconsolable.

During this time, Fran became my rock. "Your mother lived to be a doting mother and then a grandmother. Consider yourself fortunate to have had such a totally charming, gentle and incredible mother for as long as you did."

Many people admired her and welcomed her as a friend. The funeral parlor overflowed with the people she had been able to help, people I did not even know. She was interred in the cemetery belonging to a burial society founded by the IMAS. It had been created largely through her motivation. A memorial now stands at the entrance dedicated to all the people who were murdered in Europe.

Chapter Twenty-Seven

Every day of my life I must confront the demons of my mind, or they will take over and ruin everything I have built up. These phantoms in my head sowed the seeds of mistrust in my childhood, and it seems I am forever reaping their harvest.

My past is always with me...haunting me...nudging me...reminding me of what was. And as George Eliot asked in Middlemarch, "What loneliness is more lonely than mistrust?" I know this feeling well.

In 1971, years after I returned to Massachusetts, I changed jobs from one hotel chain to another. We move to Manchester, New Hampshire, to be nearer to the chain's headquarters. My life is now more or less routine.

My job, which brings me much satisfaction, carries a great deal of responsibility. Unfortunately, my ever present survivor mechanism makes some situations stressful for me. This feeling erupts whenever I am introduced to new hotel managers. Most of them are Europeans, my age or older. I always feel cynical, mistrusting, and suspicious about who these people really are and what they may be hiding in their past.

"Be careful," those nagging phantoms whisper. "Where were you during World War II? Be cautious now. What were you doing while I was trying to escape?" My mind seems to interrogate my soul.

I still shoulder a great deal of resentment about the events which affected my father's life and mine, as well as millions of others because of the support the German people gave the Nazis. I recognize some of the people I meet professionally are old enough to have been in World War II, and they act like a trigger.

I still hear my father's voice saying, "I have taken enough crap from those brown shirted bastards." My mind discharges assumptions, and I cannot help but wonder if perhaps these people still embrace the same attitude the German POW displayed when I was having my first good American meal. Too bad we didn't get all you Jews, or how did you, a Jew, get to be an executive in such a large non-Jewish company?

In Manchester, in the 1980s, Fran and I had the good fortune to meet two charming exchange students, Jens and Joern Freydank and their parents. They were visiting from Berlin, the city where I was born. Interestingly enough my ghosts remained silent when I was in their company. I don't know whether it is their ages or…who knows? Maybe I am overcoming my biases at last. The Freydanks and I start to correspond several times a year.

People who know me understand I am deeply proud of my heritage. However, my past keeps poking its finger at me, and I get very defensive whenever I hear derogatory comments about anyone's religion, but especially when it is made by or about Jews.

"I do not appreciate self-deprecating remarks," I often tell my friends if they start to tell a joke degrading religion.

I have never been hesitant about speaking of my Jewish identity. We Jews have gone through a great deal just to survive, and I believe we should be proud of our traditions and accomplishments.

Although formally I have become less and less religiously active as I once was when our children were growing up, I believe strongly that how one practiced his or her religion is highly personal. "As long as Jews do not deny their identity, I have no quarrel with how they observe their beliefs."

In 1988, years after I had escaped from France, someone thought it would be a good idea if we held a reunion with those of us who had lived in Chabannes.

"Hey, Steve," a friendly voice greeted me when I answered the telephone. "It's me…Gerry…remember? From Chabannes."

"Sure I remember. You were the one who had his bicycle under the window and…"

He interrupted. "You remember all right. The reason I'm calling is…"

And he started to tell me several "alumni" have been in touch with one another and thought it would be interesting to get together and visit "the old homestead."

"It's a thought. I'll get back to you soon, Gerry. Nice talking to you."

I mulled over the idea of returning to a place that had few happy memories. On the other hand…

"What do you think?" I ask Fran.

"If you believe it will not be too much of an emotional strain on you, I say, let's go for it."

So, Frances and I flew to France to visit my former refuge. We were taken to the Chateau near Paris, but were not allowed to enter. It is now occupied by the French equivalent of the Counter Intelligent Corps. Nevertheless, the reunion was a huge success. To this day many of us keep in touch.

Chapter Twenty-Eight

Time passes. Our lives were pretty routine when in 1995, at the suggestion of a friend, I responded to an invitation by the German government to visit the city of Berlin. After filling out the bureaucratic paperwork I received a generous offer for an all expense paid trip for myself, my wife and one child over the age of 16.

"What do you think, Fran? Shall I take advantage of the offer? I can only guess they are doing this to try to make amends for all the damage they caused. Shall I support their notion if, in fact, that is what they are doing?"

"Sure. Why not. I know you must feel a bit nervous about going back to your past," Fran says, "but it might help get rid of those nightmares of yours. And besides, you did well when we visited France."

Her encouragement helped me decide. We decided to take our daughter Ellen, since our son had been to France with us in 1988. Much to our pleasure, our son was willing to join us at his own expense.

"I don't know if I can do this by myself," I told Fran. "Being surrounded by my family may help me feel less fearful of my demons.

"One thing I have to do even before we leave for Berlin. I must be sure the road we are to take from the airport does not go over my birth mother's original grave site."

I wrote to the Freydanks, our Berlin friends, whom we had met as an exchange students in New Hampshire and told them of our planned visit. They volunteered to be our tour guides visiting the special places I needed to see.

On May 19, we started on our trip back in time.

I did not sleep too well on the flight. My nightmares were taking over again. Will anyone make anti-Semitic remarks? Will we be welcome? Finally, sleep erases all thoughts.

When I awoke I suddenly remembered something from my past.

I am on the train with the kindertransport, and as the train crosses the border into France, I draw three x's, "xxx," on the rear platform window in the dust. In Germany this used to mean, "I will never return." Now here I am violating my own determination written on a train window as a child, so many years ago.

When I left Berlin in 1939, I was a 14-year-old with a 14-year-old's vocabulary. One of the first things I discover is my limited ability to communicate in the German language when I have difficulty at the hotel simply trying to ask for a laundry bag. Gradually, however, I manage to speak reasonably well.

I felt really nervous on our arrival. Fran, aware of my anxiety, took hold of my hand. "The past will only hurt you now if you allow it, Stephan. Remember, your family is here with you. Stay in the present, and our love will protect you."

That soothed me for the moment. Our first full day we started with a three-hour city bus tour. During the war 70% of the city had been destroyed by Allied bombing. I saw now that West Berlin was almost all rebuilt. What was once East Berlin, suffering harshly under the Russian occupation, was presently under reconstruction.

"Would you believe," our middle aged tour guide asked us, "there were so many cranes visible on the skyline, a composer wrote 'Symphony of the Cranes. And when it was performed, the crane operators participated by rotating the cranes to the rhythm of the music."

We all laughed at imagining the sight.

One of the places we visited was Ploetzensee Concentration Camp, located outside the city limits. "It was a very bad time for all of us," the tour guide says into his microphone so we all could hear. "During the war, 200 hangings of political as well as Jewish prisoners took place each day."

"He doesn't tell you," I whispered to Fran, "that after the hangings the families of those murdered were presented with invoices for the labor charges for their execution. And if the families could not pay, the Nazis liquidated their furnishings to satisfy the debt, those bastards."

"Shhhh. He'll hear you," Bert, one of our group said referring to the tour guide.

"I don't care if he does hear," I told him.

"At the time people didn't know what was happening," the tour guide continued. Hearing some murmuring in the bus the tour guide decided to remind the group he was only a toddler during the war, thereby exonerating himself. He continues, "Some people say they didn't know, but I find that hard to believe."

"Well, if they didn't know, they must have been deaf and blind with stuffing up their noses," I quietly added. I was feeling that old anger again.

"Yeah, that has always been their excuse. Another in our group mimics in a childlike sing-song tone, 'We didn't know.'"

Many in our group explain they had some guilt feelings coming back, but their curiosity got the better of them. Why I came back I don't know. Maybe to face my fears.

After the tour we drove to the City Hall where we were greeted by the Canzonnette Choir. Their selections resulted in a sing-along of songs from yesteryear. The result of the music caused tears of nostalgia among many in our group. After we were served lunch, we met Jens and his girlfriend, and my first challenging day continued.

Whoever said you can't go home again is right. What I witnessed and learned proves this adage to be true.

We located the Jewish school I had to attend after Kristallnacht now located in the onetime separate city of East Berlin. It had been totally bombed out and new apartments were being built in its place.

"See, over there," I pointed out to my family. "That is approximately the location of the school entrance where we were beaten daily by the Hitler youth with their damned steel buckled belts." I felt anger now, like molten lava oozing inside my throat. No one said anything. They just let me feel.

Next we went to Kepenicker Strasse, my home from 1925 until my first mother died in 1932. I really felt strange looking at the house number. I pointed out to Fran. "See up there, the third floor. That's where I used to lived," and I indicated the doorway where the dogs saved me from a molester.

Arthur, my son, suggested we go upstairs to see if we can gain entrance to the old apartment. We knocked on the door hoping whoever lived here would let us in.

A very surprised young man opened the door, and after we explained, he graciously allowed us to take a tour of the place. I recognized the kitchen, and in the bedroom there was a crib standing in the same place my bed stood.

"There is still no central heating," I said smiling.

"Yes," the tenant says. "Some things never change."

The building where my father had the tobacco store had been completely bombed out of existence, but his words still exist in my mind. I still can hear him sobbing as he told me, "She's gone, my son. Your mother is dead. We are all alone now."

I don't remember ever feeling as close as when we sat down together on a wooden box, hugged each other and cried.

The address where my father lived after he came out of the concentration camp in 1933 was torn down to make room for the Berlin Wall.

"Lets go back to the hotel," Fran suggested. She sensed by the way I was holding on to her that I had enough reminiscing for one day, and she was right.

The memories and emotions I was experiencing did not...no, could not touch my children who were brought up in the safety of home and country. But at least they were learning their family's history first hand.

The next day we had been invited to a reception at the American Embassy. It was there I learned about the Jewish population of present day Germany.

It is almost impossible for me to realize only about 45,000 Jews now live in Germany. Of those, 20,000 live in Berlin, 18,000 of whom are recent emigrates from Russia. *What my father would have thought had he lived to see this? Would his attitude about first being German remain the same after working for a Russian Jew?* I wonder.

After lunch we four visited the place where the orphanage I lived in once stood, and the first school I attended. In those days, before 1935, the school had accommodated both Jewish and Gentile students. I remember standing in that cold entry room as "the new one," as if it were yesterday, and the memory didn't feel good. I had an ache in the pit of my stomach.

The orphanage had been bombed out and is replaced with an apartment house. The old Jewish cemetery took a direct hit from a bomb destroying a number of graves. Nothing has been rebuilt. Where buildings of my past once stood there are now piles of bricks. We each pick up one of these bricks to take home. That is all that is left of my background—bricks and many unhappy, haunting memories.

The next day Berlin's House of Representatives sponsored an excursion boat trip on the Wannsee, where the infamous Wannsee Conference took place and where the "final solution" to kill Jews was planned. The beauty of the sun, the blue of the sky and the gentle flowing of the river cannot erase the ugliness of what transpired here.

Later we visit the Oranienburg Concentration Camp where my father was taken in 1933. Years later its name was changed to Sachsenhousen when it was turned into an extermination camp. We view a film sponsored by the Russians in which it clearly acknowledges the fact that prisoners were brought here as early as 1933.

Seeing the film about Oranienburg Concentration Camp, my rage against the German system of those days is rekindled. Although I try to hide my emotions from the others, seeing the place where my father endured hard labor, suffered physical beatings to a point of having lost all is teeth, and finally suffering his first heart attack, I feel overwhelmed with grief. The pain and anger I did not know how to verbalize, and could not have expressed as a child surged up in me like a volcano spewing lava. I try to control my feelings and hold them inside until my gut feels as if it will burst. I sit on a nearby bench and cry.

I do not blame the young German people of today, but I do condemn those living at that time who allowed such a catastrophe to happen without a whimper of protest.

The next day was Saturday, the Jewish Sabbath. After attending services, 88 survivors were individually invited to spend an afternoon with a different German family. We were invited by our friends, the Freydanks and had a great time. We ate some delicious pastry with cups of strong German coffee. I am reminded of the first time I learned about my parents' love for one another. I heard my father's voice as if he were here now.

"You like Johanna, don't you?" he asked me. When I agreed, Johanna pushed a slice of almond cake covered with thick whipped cream onto my plate. I miss her more than ever now.

Our friends offered us an invitation for dinner, but we declined. In the late afternoon we returned to our hotel, exhausted, physically, mentally and spiritually.

On Sunday we visited Jewish places in Berlin, including the synagogue in which we had attended services the day before. There we learned the building had been saved on Kristallnacht only because two apartment houses, occupied by non-Jews were connected to the structure and would also have gone up in flames.

It seemed presently living in Berlin as a Jew, at least, is a precarious business. All temples, museums and Jewish schools are guarded by the police around the clock. No one is allowed to park in front of a Jewish building unless a permit has been obtained 24 hours in advance so that additional police protection can be provided.

Our last stop was at a monument located where once a temple stood. At the location once served as the assembly point for deporting Jews to death camps were plaques in the ground naming each temple destroyed in Berlin during the Holocaust. Each deportation was carved out showing how many were deported, the date and the destination. The most disturbing date to me was April, 1945, just a few days before the war ended. There was still time to depart 24 more Jews.

The next day, after visiting a large department store, trying and failing to find a German Jewish article to bring home to our grandson, Alex, we saw a large billboard. It lists the names of all the concentration camps, reminding the people of Germany and visitors to never forget the horrors of these camps.

Before we leave I had one more glance in my personal rear view mirror. Our friends drove us 25 miles to Alt Glienicke, the town in which my first mother and her family had lived. I approached an elderly lady I see standing near where I thought my grandparents house is located.

"Ach," she said, "I knew your grandmother. She died in the 1950's. Your grandfather died a few years earlier."

She pointed out the Puls' house, and the five of us approached the front door. After explaining to the present owner about my grandparents, the amazed occupant graciously let us in.

Thus ended a painful chapter in my book of memories. We left for home the next day.

Chapter Twenty-Nine

In 1993, two years before my family and I visited Germany, I started a new type of pursuit. I had just retired when my family and I went to see *Schindler's List* and were very moved by the film. Little did I know how that film would change my life.

My new journey started a short time after seeing the film, *Schindler's List* . Some friends, including a young teacher from our local high school and others my age, all American born, met over coffee and started asking me questions about my past experiences. After our discussion the teacher approached me.

"Stephan, I was born after the war, and I don't know nor can I imagine what you and the people endured under the Nazi regime. Have you ever thought of sharing your experiences with high school students?"

"Do you think they will really be interested?"

"I definitely do. Let me talk with my principal, and I'll get back to you."

My school teacher friend called and was so enthused about her suggestion when I answered the phone she yelled her elated "YES."

"Yes, what?" I asked her.

"Stephan, the principal is so excited when I told him about you. He wants to schedule a meeting with you in one of the classes."

And that is how I began to talk to various school classes in New England and a few in San Diego about my experiences growing up in Nazi Germany and in Nazi occupied France. Most of the responses I have received have been most gratifying, but not all.

One instructor of an eighth grade class criticized me in front of his class for "being biased."

I replied, "Sir, there is no other way I could possible be." The children actually applauded. This remark was at least partially responsible for my decision to make the trip to Berlin my family and I took two years later.

Perhaps repeating my story over and over is a sort of therapy. I know I have fewer nightmares.

I have received all types of reactions in letters, some were written by children old beyond their years, beautiful, upsetting and sensitive.

The most childlike but honest letter I received was from a young grammar school student.

> Mr. Lewy, I thoght your presentation was interesting as well as yar persinality enjoyable. Thogh a tad boring at time, it was Fun and I'm sure you can spice it up a little any ways. Thank you.

A very different and disturbing letter was written by a junior high school student.

Dear Mr. Lewy,

> Hi, my name is (Lola). I enjoyed your speech today about what it was like for you during the war. I thought that it was fascinating to hear the story of a Jewish person that lived through the war. Over the last month I have done two interviews with two different people from (Farnsworth) about what life was like for them during the war but that was the American side. Last year my brother and a few of his friends started hanging out with people who thought blacks and Jews should be killed and that Hitler rule over all. In January (of last year) a black kid named (Artie) moved into the house next door to us, my brother and his friends beat him up. Now the boys (who did it) are going through the legal system. I was shocked because I didn't realize that my brother could do that, especially in my town

of (Farnsworth), New Hampshire. I think that it is great that you are talking to students about this and educating them.

Thank you.

The most moving letter I received was from an eighth grade girl.

Dear M. Lewy,

Thank you for coming and telling us about your life history. I didn't understand some of your words because I am from Albania and I have been working with English for only 2 month. From you I learned more about the Holocaust and Jewish people. In Albania the same thing happened as in the Holocaust "in Germany." The president of Albania was like Hitler. They had the same rules, and the president wanted to kill people without reason. If you talk to people and said anything about president or the regime, the people who listen to you would go and tell the police about you in secret. Then the police come to your house and take you in to the jail or they take you to court and you have a meeting with the president or government. Then the president or government asks you questions. The president or government tells you: this is the end, and they kill you. I told you this story because I want you to know that I have seen in my life, problem like this. I was very emotional when I was listening to you because for a moment I thought of my grandfather in Albania. My grandfather is the same age as you are and he lived a fearful life more years ago. He couldn't talk about what he was thinking and he couldn't get a good job because the rules were very strict. Now he still live in Albania with his wife but soon he is coming in U.S.A. and I am writing for him and my grandmother. Now he is very happy for us and for himself, because we can live a life of freedom and without mistrust and brutality. I am very happy that I can see the people in Albania living

a life with freedom because the old regime is gone.
I tell you thank you for coming! It was very nice for me to
listen to someone like you!
With respect
(Signed)

Somehow a letter like this and the hundreds of others I receive make any effort I make seem worthwhile.

In my talks I sometimes refer to Sam Levinson's answer to an anti-Semite. It seems to make a lasting impression of the school children and their teacher.

"Humanitarian consistency requires that my people offer all these gifts to all people of the world. Fanatic consistency requires that all bigots accept Syphilis, Diabetes, Convulsions, Malnutrition, Infantile Paralysis (Polio) and Tuberculosis as a matter of principal."

The trip to my past urges me on. Where the structures of my background once stood, there are now ruins—piles of bricks symbolizing what might have been. An ancient seventeenth century Jewish sage, Ball Shem Tov, said, "Remembrance is the secret of redemption." Although I'll never forget the past, the time has come for me to remain in the present, to do what I am able to do. I have had my vendetta—my revenge. When I look into the children's faces listening to my story, there is hope I can make a difference—make them more open minded, less judgmental, and more grateful for living in America. My vendetta is to make these children aware of how priceless freedom is.

Printed in the United States
27533LVS00001B/213